DYING TO LIVE:

The Christian's Pathway to Experiencing God More Deeply

Charles
Jn 12:24

BY CHARLES HALEY

DEDICATION

*To Life Serve associates for their patience in reading
what I don't have time to say when we meet.*

*To those who are living with bruised lives or broken
hearts and are finding greatness of life and soul as
they do.*

ACKNOWLEDGEMENT

*To Stan Guthrie for sharing his well-honed skills apart
from which the product would be markedly less.*

DYING TO LIVE:
The Christian's Pathway to Experiencing God More Deeply
by Charles Haley

INTRODUCTION – **Learning That Living Requires Dying**

PART ONE – **PERSONAL LESSONS**

1. **The Gospels & The Principle of Planting**

2. **Abraham: Giving Up What Your Life Is All About**

PART TWO – **Marketplace Lessons**

12. Job: Destroyed By Disasters and Restored

13. Habakkuk: Dying to My National Expectations

14. Moses: Learning to Die after Extreme Living and Leadership

15. Joseph and the Dungeon

16. The Choice

✖ ✖ ✖

Learning That Living Requires Dying

Dying is a normal daily part of physical life.
Continual dying is also a normal part of spiritual life –
a discipline that we learn through painful experience.

DYING TO LIVE PRINCIPLE
What you hold back holds you hostage.

Americans don't talk about death much, because we fear it, but it's pretty obvious that we're fixated on the subject. We pursue elaborate and costly approaches to healthcare, we pay big money for unproven elixirs, and we talk about "passing away" rather than the more honest "dying." While focusing as much as possible on our busy day to day existence, death is always lurking around the corner.

Because we have become so advanced medically and scientifically, we have forgotten or suppressed the fact that dying is a normal, even daily part of physical life. No matter our circumstances or age, each day we live brings us one day closer to our deaths. And by the time we reach the ripe old age of 30, our bodies have begun to remind us of what is ahead, through increasingly frequent aches, pains, breakdowns, and diseases.

Many people, however, attempt to sustain their lives without grasping the fundamental principles of living. In late 2009, the well-connected president of the Chicago School Board found his life experience unbearable. His body was found in the Chicago River. Every year yields a similar harvest of dark, irrevocable hopelessness for many.

Yet we who are wise and brave will face death squarely, knowing that it is an integral part of life. As Shakespeare wrote:

Cowards die many times before their deaths;
The valiant never taste of death but once.
Of all the wonders that I yet have heard,
It seems to me most strange that men should fear;
Seeing that death, a necessary end,
Will come when it will come.

If you are living, you are already dying. When you stop dying, you are no longer living. The president of the United States, who has reached the pinnacle, is paying the price with his life. The couch potato who works every day for couch time—beer, sports, and fast food—is dying to live. The model mother or father, church member, or civic-minded volunteer is likewise dying to live. Our first parents guaranteed that every human being to follow would inherit this process. Every one of us experiences death in order to live.

Yes, death is a part of physical life. And the prospect of death helps us live better lives now. Knowing the brevity of life helps us to remember to make the most of each passing day. It helps us care for our bodies, that our pleasure and usefulness can be maximized. It helps us with priorities. It helps us keep the main thing the main thing.

But did you know that death is also a part of a healthy and balanced spiritual life—or should be? The apostle Paul recognized this simple truth with these crystal-clear words: "I have been crucified with Christ. It is no longer I who live, but Christ who lives in me. And the life I now live in the flesh I live by faith in the Son of God, who loved me and gave himself for me."[1]

Yet it is one thing to assent to the truth of this verse and others like it. It is another entirely to honestly explore what dying means to one's spiritual life. Part of the reason is that dying can be very painful. Dying this kind of death involves, just as it did for Paul, letting go of your dreams and whatever else in this world that you think confers significance on your existence.

I have experienced the painfulness of this kind of death, which is necessary if we are to live by faith in the Son of God. When I was an adolescent, I went at life the wrong way. I bought my first drink in a teenage nightclub, got my family's six-cylinder Plymouth up to 100 miles an hour on the down slope of a hill, and experimented with second rate dating patterns. I remember staring out my window into the darkness on numerous Sunday evenings, after failing to find anything life-giving over the weekend.

I was eventually forced to begin my own journey in a much different manner. Eventually I would understand that dying while living was a consistent reality and more like a companion or substrata of my life than simply an isolated circumstance here and there.

When I finally came to the Lord in irrevocable fashion at age 17, I began to claw my way up the mountain of Christian experience as I understood it. Over the years, however, the sense that hung over my head was that I could never do enough, accomplish what I should, or turn my failures into successes.

A rather unspectacular encounter helped me to conclude that the dying experiences of my life were more than frag-

---

1   Gal. 2:20, ESV. Unless otherwise noted, all Scripture references are taken from the New American Standard Bible.

mented episodes. This occurred recently when I met with my spiritual director on Chicago's North Side. Spiritual directors are mature, well-balanced Christians who use their sessions to help people like me to think through our lives and align them more fully with how God is working in their lives. This spiritual director characteristically was able to peer deeply into my life.

In her office I launched into a long soliloquy, dealing first with my relationship to the family, and then my journey with God. She listened patiently until I finished. Then she asked, "Do you know that the answer to everything you said could be summed up in one word?" Somewhat taken aback, I replied, "No, what is it?" Her answer: *presence*.

Just *presence?* Not my "leadership"? Not my agenda, which I have sometimes pushed for my now adult children and their families' good? My spiritual director was gently saying that I needed to step back from actively trying to manage the lives of my loved ones and simply be available to them. I could let God be God in the lives of these dear people. Absorbing the word *presence* and applying it to the role I needed to take now involved a sort of death to my expectations to more fully allow God to be God.

Our children are in their 40s, and I should have gotten this message long before. But it is a message that attacks my pride. That's because my momentum is no longer needed to help carry my family along to sustained relationships now that we number 25 people. If that phase of my life is over and done with—*dead*—where then do I fit? My spiritual counselor had told me, and I quickly realized that she was right.

The greatest gift, the best encouragement I can provide my family is through my unconditional love–and simply being available. Being present is not a mere concession, either. It is the *best* choice, and it will position me from now on to contribute whenever I *am* asked for my counsel. But make no mistake, no matter how nicely stated or how attractive my new resolve is, *it is still a form of dying to what is past.*

As painful as this meeting was, it prompted a form of dying that I needed. It was good for me to finally grasp that God was not limited to my many limitations, warps, and shortcomings. My thick skull figured out that maybe it is all right to step back a little. And this incident opened my eyes to the fact that we must die as often as the Lord brings problem areas to light.

Well, that was quite enough dying for one meeting, but I wasn't finished yet. My spiritual director continued her gentle probing. How did *presence* apply to the rest of my Christian life?

"Charles," she said, "the Lord knows you have struggled, that you have given your best effort and often failed. He knows that your deepest desire is to know, love and serve God. Now, just be *present* to your heavenly Father, rest on Him who gives rest and receive the love of Him who loves you because of what He is, not what you are."

There it was again–a call to another step of dying. It began to dawn on me that dying, letting go of my dreams, having my hopes pried out of my ego-centered grip was part and parcel of my experience. Now I was being called to let go again and be with God. I was forced to acknowledge that I was naked before God, stripped of all my supposed ability to perform and do. This realization sparked an extended period of self-examination.

I remember the internal pressure I have felt over the years when I defaulted to comparing myself to my seminary mates who became well known and powerful leaders. I further descended into anger, resentment or bitterness. As the years passed, I began to realize the amazing way in which my life had been blessed. Even then, without really knowing why, I was reluctant or even a little afraid to confront this terrific reality. I always felt a sense of brokenness that seemed to relegate me to a second-tier life and ministry.

During my deliberations, I decided to create a list of the things that had bruised my life or broken my heart. Though I hadn't known it, these things had contributed to my dying even as God was lovingly intervening. Six areas came to mind quickly. Each can still draw emotional blood.

Since my conversion, I had lived with a relentless passion, no matter how badly I was beaten up, beaten down or kicked around. My passion was to become a strategic Christian leader able to touch thousands of lives and reach far beyond the United States. I thirsted after highly leveraged Christian leadership.

Yet it seemed that this goal was always just out of reach. Yes, there were special times along these lines, but they never lasted. I had a four-year stint as dean of education in a Christian Bible college. I taught a wonderful array of courses, led the faculty, developed curricula, and preached in churches as an academic leader.

Even during this very fulfilling period, I was in a tenuous position. The small school was on the financial rocks and eventually folded. I was pushed out and landed as a correctional chaplain. Even though I spearheaded an outreach to prisoners in India, traveled widely there, and conducted Bible conferences, this was a difficult and financially stressed period of time.

I longed for a place to stand, a venue in which I could use, develop and maximize the gifts and passions that had been entrusted to me. During this time, I dreaded what I saw in

Hebrews 11. *My section* was preceded by great incidences of conquest, heroism and deliverance. Then comes the pit!

> Others suffered mocking and flogging, and even chains and imprisonment. They were stoned, they were sawn in two, they were killed with the sword. They went about in skins of sheep and goats, destitute, afflicted, mistreated—of whom the world was not worthy—wandering about in deserts and mountains, and in dens and caves of the earth.[2]

Wandering in deserts and mountains and caves caught my eye. It was the idea of being unsettled–no place to take a stand–just wandering, that I reluctantly identified with. These saints were stripped of what is considered normal, what makes for a fulfilling life. During this period, I prayed, "Lord, if this is your call on my life, I hate the idea. I pray that it is not what you have chosen for me. Yet, if that is your highest and best will for me, I accept it." It was another opportunity to die to my dreams and plans.

But, like all death, it was painful, and I was in consternation over losing my dreams. One day I told my wife, Jo Ann, "I am going out to howl at the moon." My venue was an abandoned gravel pit. I began my session with an apology. "Lord, I am sorry for what I am about to say but it's the way it is with me right now. I know you are my heavenly Father, and it hurts to think about what I am about to say to you."

Now in the six verses of Psalm 13, the Psalmist goes through three two-verse stages. In the first, he rather insultingly asks how long the Lord is going to forget him. In the next stage,

---

2   Heb. 11:36-38, ESV.

he begins to recover his equilibrium with a more reasonable prayer. In the final two verses, his heart soars skyward with joy, gratefulness and exaltation. On this day, however, I got no further than stage one. My heart did not rise in gratefulness for how wonderful God had been to me in the past. I was hurt, angry and frustrated.

So I began to shout at the Lord, "How long are you going to kick me around? Why don't you shoot me in the head or heart? Are you going to let me lie in a mud puddle the rest of my life and just walk over me? Why don't you just shoot me and get it over with?"

After bellowing all this out, I sat quietly, legs dangling over the edge of the pit, and waited. Then I got up and went home. Now, several years later, I remember sharing the grief, tears or rage of other men who in one way or another were enduring a similar stage of life. The obvious question is, "Why?" That is what the rest of the book is about! We will tap into a stream of experience and truth in the Bible that is both tough and transforming–a framework in which we can view some of life's most formidable and heart-breaking experiences.

Before we plunge into the rest of this book, however, let's go back to Hebrews 11. In verse 38, note what is said about these saints wandering in deserts, mountains, and caves. They are described as those "of whom the world was not worthy." This little statement is unique in all of Scripture. These days, I come to these words in wonderment and awe–as if I am stepping into a sacred shrine. *Saints of whom the world is not worthy* is an astonishing truth. These people—who were the offscouring, the rejects of society, those to be pitied—receive an honor without parallel in Scripture. The world was not worthy to receive their footprints! These pitiable wanderers are given a stratospheric status!

After some years, I have been able to get my arms around my own life and pray with genuine, although perhaps not perfect, honesty, "Lord, as long as you had plenty of candidates to be prominent Christians–international organizational leaders, pastors of large and strategic churches, influential writers whose books sold many thousands of copies and made them headliners at great conferences–I am grateful you withheld this from me. Getting glimpses of the height and extent of your plan for my life is stunning and many times more than sufficient ... and I haven't even understood much of it yet!" And when grief or sorrow, anger or regret contaminate my heart, I am also never without a sense of awe regarding the unfolding story which is transcending what caused my pain in the past.

When I revisit the abandoned gravel pit, I can begin to say with Job, "I have declared that which I did not understand . . . and I repent in dust and ashes."[3] Had I received everything I wanted, I would have missed out on essential growth in my spiritual life.

Looking from the outside into the circumstances of another, I don't understand how Job survived his ordeal. I comprehend even less how the desolate, unsupported, vagabond people of Hebrews 11 pulled through. And yet they did. If you told me about some frighteningly dark period of your life, I might secretly wonder how you would make it. However, like Job and the amazing people we have considered from Hebrews, I believe you will! How?

It involves holding your hopes and dreams with an open hand. It is all about dying, not to die, but to live.

---

3   Job 42:3, 6.

DYING TO LIVE APPLICATION

Consider the things that have deeply disappointed you or broken your heart and tell God of your intention and desire to trust him despite these disappointments.

QUESTIONS FOR REFLECTION

With your own life disappointments, heartbreaks or broken dreams in mind:

How do you respond to God?

Can you discover any benefits?

Are there raw and painfully broken areas of your life that persist?

PART ONE

Personal Lessons

✠ ✠ ✠

CHAPTER 1

The Gospels & the Principle of Planting

DYING TO LIVE PRINCIPLE
Submit to the process of planting that Jesus requires.

Every spring, a maple tree close to our property line drops thousands of helicopter-like seeds. They pirouette down, covering the newly awakened grass. They clog gutters. They pile up by the steps leading into our home. Another tree, a cottonwood, launches delicate, airborne fluff balls. By the millions they pile up inches deep and make patches of the ground appear weirdly snow-covered.

Downstate from Chicago, in the Corn Belt, green and yellow John Deere tractors pull planters, some of which plant 36 or more rows at a time. They run all day long, sometimes all night with changes of drivers. Equipped with GPS devices, they traverse the huge fields with laser-like accuracy. The result eventually is a harvest that feeds millions of hungry people, most of whom have no idea where their sustenance comes from.

Whether by a helicopter diving into your moist backyard soil or a shiny combine, the laws of planting and harvesting remain the same, as they have since the dawn of civilization. We must drop the plough into the darkness and depth, where seeds go to germinate, grow, and be harvested.

Germination is a complex area of plant biology. It varies widely from species to species and plant to plant. The third verse of John's Gospel claims that "all things came into being through Him, and apart from Him nothing came into being that has come into being." He is the Author of this wonder, which is encased in the fabulous array of seeds that produce the plants that carpet the earth. Scientists continue to research the rich and ever-unfolding secrets of seed germination.

While an entire book could only provide an introduction to seed biology, our Lord reduces this sobering yet transforming concept to its essence.

"Truly, truly, I say to you, unless a grain of wheat falls into the earth and dies, it remains alone; but if it dies, it bears much fruit."[4]

His analogy involves a seed. The seed has an outer husk and an embryo inside. For new life to occur, something must happen to this outer covering. It has to be damaged, made rotten, or in some way broken down to free the living but dormant germ or nucleus within.

For eighteen months, this verse was never far from my thinking. When taken in context, this statement separates the essential from the peripheral. It is critical in helping us grasp a law of the spiritual life that underlies both the Old and New Testaments–dying to live.

The verse falls in the middle of a chapter over which the pall of death hangs heavily. We are reminded three times of Lazarus' recent dying and raising from the dead. The chapter opens with Mary lavishing her extraordinarily expensive perfume on the Lord. With her keen perception and passionate heart, this devoted disciple knows what is coming–his death.

---

4   John 12:24.

After describing a plot to kill Lazarus, the narrative continues with Jesus' triumphal entry and the hardened opposition of the Pharisees. Then we meet some Greeks, who have come to Jerusalem to worship. In contrast to the Lord's opponents, the Greeks seek an audience with him. Yet we find everything focusing on his death. Jesus responds that the hour of his death and consequent glorification has come.

With the shadow of the cross darkening the path ahead, Jesus turns aside the request of the Greek worshipers. Let's look at this passage in some detail, and the verse in context, for the principle they declare is foundational to all that lies ahead in our study. Our theme verse occurs in the dead center.

Now there were some Greeks among those who were going up to worship at the feast; these then came to Philip, who was from Bethsaida of Galilee, and began to ask him, saying, "Sir, we wish to see Jesus." Philip came and told Andrew; Andrew and Philip came and told Jesus. And Jesus answered them, saying, "The hour has come for the Son of Man to be glorified. Truly, truly, I say to you, unless a grain of wheat falls into the earth and dies, it remains alone; but if it dies, it bears much fruit. He who loves his life loses it, and he who hates his life in this world will keep it to life eternal. If anyone serves Me, he must follow Me; and where I am, there My servant will be also; if anyone serves Me, the Father will honor him. "Now My soul has become troubled; and what shall I say, 'Father, save Me from this hour'? But for this purpose I came to this hour."[5]

---

5   John 12:20-27.

John 12 is about dying, ours included. Jesus was troubled at the prospect of his death as the hour approached, as we are troubled about ours. Yet he spoke clearly of his dying as the reason he came to earth.

In a similar way, our life purpose also cannot be fulfilled without our dying. This truth is unavoidable, and it is placed at the heart of this chapter. To reject this principle is akin to spurning Christ's death for us. Jesus says essentially that if we refuse to die, we won't live, either.

Generations ago, my forebears homesteaded farmland in central Illinois, and the harvests were labor-intensive. Today, with more efficient and powerful equipment, it is not unusual for farmers to get 200 bushels of corn per acre. I have seen a million bushels of corn being stored outdoors when the grain elevators were full. I find the billions of golden kernels heaped high in the sunshine to be strikingly beautiful. However, each one is a result of the harsh natural law our Lord refers to in John 12:24: *unless a grain of wheat falls into the earth and dies, it remains alone; but if it dies, it bears much fruit.* The spectacular sight of tons of exquisitely shaped kernels is merely the visible side of the invisible *dying* process to which our Lord refers.

A portion of the huge corn harvest in the Midwest is reserved for seed corn. The next harvest can only take place after this highest quality corn is prepared, planted, and nurtured in the rich soil and ideal climate. During the summer, thousands of acres will exhibit lush, green stalks that grow as high as or higher than a man and stand in geometrically straight and spaced rows.

Every ear of corn can have upwards of 400 kernels or more. It is the result of a uniform law of reproduction. The outer husk of the planted kernel will degenerate and partially decompose. Its former beauty and symmetry are lost to a rotting, and life-producing, process. This process must happen every time because the germinating kernel within is hidden inside the external husk—the part we can see. The husk, which to the untrained eye appears so complete, must be sacrificed for what is essential within.

This death-before-life process is directly applicable to the Christian. We also have external and internal aspects to our lives. The external often seems important, even consuming: how we look, what we do, our status or standing, our resources, our relationships. We make it our business to conserve, preserve and steward the outer components of our lives—the husk.

- Undergraduate or graduate studies help position us in our careers.
- Hard work pays off with a stable income and promotions, which supposedly guarantee that our goals in life can be met.
- Medical insurance makes the treatment of our physical ills affordable.
- Vacations and travel enrich our families.

But the principle of the corn kernel puts all these outward things of life in their proper place. Any aspect of our external lives, no matter how good or pleasurable, is in God's hands. He can remove it—bury it, crush it, allow it to rot—for his own good purposes, if he deems it necessary for our growth. The beautiful expressions of a desirable lifestyle can no more be held as ends in themselves than a kernel of seed corn can be preserved without planting. The divinely implanted kernel of life—resulting from the work of Christ on our behalf and transmitted by the Holy Spirit—is to be nurtured, developed, and released, whatever that may mean to the husk. We cannot always see this process at work in other people. We need to remember not to judge by external appearances. A beautiful woman may hold her beauty far more loosely than a plain female counterpart who marshals her vanity to look better than anyone else in her office. The kernel phases are observable and scientifically verifiable, but the internalized principle of dying to live in a human being may be completely hidden to us.

Origen of Alexandria highlights the profound problem we face as frail human beings who have come into relationship with the eternal God. This third-century saint noted how we are enveloped in our own darkness, as authors Richard J. Foster and Gayle D. Beebe summarize his thought: "The greatest challenge we face is not lack of belief but the enormous gravity of our egocentric desires. The weight of these desires creates a force on human nature that is virtually impossible to escape."[6]

Our Lord gives us an answer to this tragic conundrum in his death-dealing yet liberating pronouncement in John 12:24. The natural analogy is raised to a higher power. It is no longer an outer husk that must degenerate, rot and expose the living kernel hidden inside. It is what is native to our human state—behavior patterns, attitudes and mode of living—that must be broken open, shattered or reordered. Only then will our lives be released from our own tomblike existence. We must die in order to live.

Yet in us this unseen process differs from the germination cycle that begins with a planted seed in the springtime and

---

6   Richard J. Foster and Gayle D. Beebe, *Longing for God: Seven Paths of Christian Devotion* (Downers Grove, IL: InterVarsity Press, 2009), 23.

ends with a fall harvest. I came to realize this when I felt stabbed with grief while reflecting on Origen's insight. Why was I reacting this way? I was becoming aware of the "enormous gravity of my egocentric desires" for a visible, strategic ministry career.

So I asked myself two questions. The first was, "Is your loss real?" The honest answer: "Yes. It hurts and along with other losses, my heart has been shredded along the way!" The second was, "Is my life any less at its most essential level?" The answer: "No. On the contrary, I sense an interior freeing, of being alive in Christ–of being able to say inwardly, 'I share your life somehow, and everything else is negotiable and dispensable. If my deeply felt desires were to stand in the way of this reality and relationship, I would gladly give them up.'"

The kernel of our lives is deeper, more genuine and compelling than the surface things that break our hearts. Yes, my loss is real. I *do* feel the pain deeply, but I remind myself that it is evidence only of a shattered husk. Its brokenness and degeneration remind me of what is essential–the living kernel of life in Christ, from which the miracle of a greening life and multigenerational productivity can spring.

The Apostle Paul experienced this death-before-life process, too.

> Always carrying about in the body the dying of Jesus, so that the life of Jesus also may be manifested in our body. For we who live are constantly being delivered over to death for Jesus' sake, so that the life of Jesus also may be manifested in our mortal flesh. So death works in us.[7]

---

7   2 Corinthians 4:10-12.

A genuine experience with God involves dying. However it may come or in whatever circumstances, we cannot embody the deeply formed life the Lord describes without having elements of our outer lives stripped away in a kind of death.

So then, John 12:24 becomes the springboard from which the rest of our study follows.

"Truly, truly, I say to you, unless a grain of wheat falls into the earth and dies, it remains alone; but if it dies, it bears much fruit."

And the process, as painful and powerful as it is, certainly does not end in this life. The seed analogy of John 12:24 culminates in the spectacular crescendo of I Corinthians. To deny the existential, dark and sometimes dirty process now is a practical repudiation of the great finale described in the following passage.

So also is the resurrection of the dead. It is sown a perishable body, it is raised an imperishable body; it is sown in dishonor, it is raised in glory; it is sown in weakness, it is raised in power; It is sown a natural body, it is raised a spiritual body. If there is a natural body, there is also a spiritual body. So also it is written, "The first Man, Adam, became a living soul." The last Adam became a life-giving spirit. However, the spiritual is not first, but the natural; Then the spiritual. The first man is from the earth, earthy; the second man is from Heaven. As is the earthy, so also are those who are earthy; and as is the heavenly, so also are those who are heavenly. Just as we have borne the image of the earthy, we will also bear the image of the heavenly.[8]

---

8   I Corinthians 15:42-49.

A hippie's apocryphal statement (said to have been recorded on a gravestone) is clever but incomplete: "Don't dig me this time, I'm really gone." We followers of Christ need to die, not when our physical lives run out, but *today*. We need to be "really gone" to the external things that keep us from experiencing the life-giving kernel of faith.

God help us to die *now*, that our lives might put another exclamation point behind the resurrection life of the risen Christ. And may we hold even the best, most cherished parts of our external husks with open hands, knowing that he wants to give us so much more.

DYING TO LIVE APPLICATION

Place "planting to live" over your losses.

QUESTIONS FOR REFLECTION

As you have looked over your list of life's injuries again, do some leave a gaping and seemingly unpluggable hole in your life? Do any of these areas still make you feel denuded or stripped of what is important to your sense of wholeness or well-being?

Is it possible that in some mysterious way your losses make your life in God and in the world more complete? If so, do you know how?

Read Colossians 3:2-4 (out loud if possible) in which the Apostle Paul provides a post-resurrection perspective on John 12:24. Are you willing to have this principle as a deeply present part of your life?

✠ ✠ ✠

CHAPTER 2

Abraham: Giving Up What Your Life Is All About

DYING TO LIVE PRINCIPLE
Go all the way with God.

If you were asked, "What is your biggest fear? What would be the most terrible loss you can imagine? What would you like to avoid at any cost?" How might you answer? You have your list of special dreads, and I have mine. Sometimes these dreads lurk in the shadows like baggage packed away in our inner closets, while we indulge in seasons of special delight. Yet in our hearts we whisper, "God is probably going to bring along something bad. He wouldn't want me to enjoy life like this for too long."

Abraham and Sarah's worst dread no doubt centered around Isaac. Abraham had received the greatest promises ever offered by the eternal God. But they could only be fulfilled through Isaac. Today, 4,000 years later, over 2 billion people still call this man from Ur of the Chaldees "Father Abraham." He would never have received this august title if he were not first the father of Isaac.

In Genesis 21, Abraham and Sarah are finally able to enjoy a relatively stable period in their nomadic existence. The stressors that had disrupted life are minimal. It is easy to imagine this old married couple having long conversations reviewing their amazing lives during this sunset period of their experience.

All the while, Abraham and Sarah take delight in Isaac, the miracle son of their old age and the culmination of their life journey. Perhaps the boy and Abraham take long walks, with the back and forth conversation producing spiritual foundation stones in Isaac's character. Abraham has settled a domestic crisis involving Sarah, the servant woman, Hagar, and his surrogate son, Ishmael. Additionally, Abraham and Abimelech have made a peace covenant, and the old saint has planted a tamarisk tree at Beersheba, calling upon the name of the Lord. How relieved Abraham would be if his sojourn were ended right here with the familiar words, "And he lived happily ever after."

Looking at Abraham, the person and the pilgrim, brings my own experience into focus. Perhaps like Abraham and Sarah in their later years, we have enjoyed blessings for which we have no explanation. My very long (but still incomplete) list would include great family blessings, spectacular travel, special fulfillment through my current ministry in which I provide leveraged growth opportunities spiritually, professionally and personally to company owners and presidents—along with all the regular delights and pleasures I enjoy in the normal routine of life. I have sometimes asked, "Why, Lord, are you pouring out this torrent of undeserved blessings? All I can do is accept them gratefully, as your feeble follower."

But this wonderful period was not to last. Like the 2010 earthquake in Haiti, the major seismic shock of Abraham's life occurred without warning.

Now it came about after these things, that God tested Abraham, and said to him "Abraham!" And he said, "Here I am." He said, "Take now your son, your only son, whom you love, Isaac, and go to the land of Moriah, and offer him there as a burnt offering on one of the mountains of which I will tell you."[9]

Instantly, Abraham's wonderful season of life shatters into a million pieces. Did his mind go numb as he is confronted with his greatest dread? Maybe it was good that he didn't take a long time to process the devastating command.

The next indescribably sad verse says it all.

So Abraham rose early in the morning and saddled his donkey, and took two of his young men with him and Isaac his son; and he split wood for the burnt offering, and arose and went to the place of which God had told him.[10]

Abraham at this point could have been forgiven for asking, "Lord, couldn't you have done this another way?" I know that this would have been my instinctive reaction. Had Abraham and Sarah been less mature, they might have said to the Lord, "You could have had anything but Isaac. We are old and could have dealt with you taking either of us. Is this what we get after leaving our homeland, spending our lives living in tents, and waiting all these years for a son? What possible benefit could there be in offering him as a human sacrifice? You have preserved us and extended mercy all the years since we left Ur. We are grateful beyond what we could ever express for knowing you. Why this? Why now? Lord, this is inconceivable. You must have a cruel sense of humor."

Now with a dagger thrust into his heart, Abraham is being asked by the Most Holy One to stick a knife into Isaac. Then he will have to watch the life blood of the son he loves more than

9   Gen. 22:1-2.
10   Gen. 22:3.

anything else drain onto the rocky terrain at the top of the terrible mountain. No emotional sedative is offered. The scene is already as bad as possible. A final twist of the knife is added when his staunch and loyal son says, "Father, everything is here but the lamb for sacrifice. Where is it?"

The plot continues in horrific fashion. Abraham ties up Isaac like a human lamb on the mountain altar. Then Abraham grabs his knife, ready to bury it into the chest of his beloved Isaac. At this moment, any Jew or Gentile reading this narrative might ask whether there is anything holy or redeeming in this incident.

As much as you and I might wish to avoid looking at this episode, we must realize that Abraham's acquiescence to God's command tells us a lot about God and about people who journey with him. What does this 4,000-year-old incident reveal about God? Most succinctly, it tells us that God is God. He can do whatever he wants. But this is good news, because he is always right and without fail acts according to his perfect character.

However, what actually happens may temporarily be inscrutable and wrapped up in a bloody, cruel package. A "quotable quote" from Yogi Berra in a coffee house newspaper says, "In theory, there is no difference between theory and practice. But in practice, there is." What we know of God in neatly tied theological constructs can be savagely tried in practice.

Anyone can give a half-dozen examples of senseless suffering—the child born with a disability, a marriage torn apart by infidelity—that seem to indicate the exact opposite, that God can be an unfeeling monster. But in Genesis 22:11-12, God is quickly revealed as the Divine Lover of an old man who has trekked his heart-breaking journey up the mountain. With

Isaac atop the wood pile and the knife ready to kill him, a new command is given.

> But the angel of the Lord called to him from heaven and said, "Abraham, Abraham!" And he said, "Here I am." He said, "Do not stretch out your hand against the lad, and do nothing to him; for now I know that you fear God, since you have not withheld your son, your only son, from Me."

God's response to Abraham is not unlike the wife who tells her husband, "I always wondered if you really loved me. Now I know." The Lord says, in one of the most sacred interchanges in all of Scripture, "now I know that you fear God, since you have not withheld your son, your only son, from Me." How many spouses are left to wonder about this all their lives, "How much does he *really* love me?"

Perhaps we can respond, "Lord, I wonder that you in all of your omniscience would want in some sense to *know* that I love you more than anything else. I hear your words to the old man, who has just met the supreme test of his life. I am afraid to ask you to help me love you that deeply … but lead on."

What am I to learn from the broken-hearted old man who labored up the mountain? Simply this: Temporal blessings are just that. And it is well worth losing them if God has judged this plan to be the highest and best. If Isaac had to be taken, then let it be so, even though any rational explanation may escape my limited understanding.

To hold onto the lesser blessing and miss the greater one is indefensible. While God can do all things, there is something he cannot do: He cannot give blessings that are better than who he is. God's plan for us is always his Plan A. While his program for Abraham was enveloped in a dark and terrible mystery, it revealed that Abraham was willing to plunge his knife into the chest of his beloved son in a test of radical obedience. While this trial put to death every expectation of blessing Abraham had ever experienced, it was also a passport to a level of greatness still celebrated today.

Several elements come together when God brings a daughter or son to this degree of trust.

- *A time of preparation.* Abraham logged many years of service after God called him to leave his homeland. He was 100 when Isaac was finally born, with many years of living with God behind him. Abraham had learned over a long period to answer God's call. He does it twice in Genesis 22. It was "here I am" when God called on him to prepare Isaac for sacrifice. When God called him on top of the mountain, he again responded with a simple "here I am." Answering the call, reporting for duty, or simply showing up is something we must learn over and over. As Woody Allen purportedly said, "Ninety percent of life is just showing up." It is a prelude to the defining moments of our lives.

- *Stripped of the peripherals.* The third "here I am" is easy to overlook. It comes when Isaac questions him on the mountain.[11] You can feel Abraham's heart in his simple response, "Here I am, my son." There is a hint here of the reality that those who have been stripped naked of the peripherals of life can be present with someone else at a deep and authentic level.

---

11   Gen. 22:7-8.

- *Faith*. When Isaac asks his pitiful, desolating question, "Dad, where is the lamb?" Abraham answers with a faith from deep within his being: "God will provide for Himself the lamb for the burnt offering, my son." Against all odds, God had taken care of him and his family for decades. Sarah was able to become pregnant and give birth to a healthy child in her 90s. This is a faith that grasps what the rational mind can't comprehend. We who follow in the footsteps of Abraham and Sarah possess a knowing deeper than our circumstances that God will provide whether we are dying, experiencing a terrible crisis at a peak time in life, or living with some other life-sapping circumstance. Abraham's awesome willingness to sacrifice Isaac can motivate us to know God similarly.

The original pronouncement of God to Abraham immediately after he was kept from sacrificing Isaac is recorded in Genesis 22:15-18.

Then the angel of the LORD called to Abraham a second time from heaven, and said, "By Myself I have sworn, declares the LORD, because you have done this thing and have not withheld your son, your only son, indeed I will greatly bless you, and I will greatly multiply your seed as the stars of the heavens and as the sand which is on the seashore; and your seed shall possess the gate of their enemies. In your seed all the nations of the earth shall be blessed, because you have obeyed My voice.

Of the many things that deserve mention, note only one: The blessings to be extended to all the nations through Abraham's seed are tied up with his willingness to sacrifice Isaac. His step of obedience was cosmic and incalculably important. Abraham's willingness to sacrifice Isaac in a single point of time had multigenerational implications.

The stream resulting from Abraham's obedience becomes the ocean of blessing in Jesus Christ, who is elsewhere referred to as the Seed of Abraham.[12]

A different perspective is given in the great pronouncement in Hebrews 11:17-19:

> By faith Abraham, when he was tested, offered up Isaac, and he who had received the promises was offering up his only begotten son; it was he to whom it was said, "In Isaac your descendants shall be called." He considered that God is able to raise people even from the dead, from which he also received him back as a type.

These two passages highlight a common theme: that Abraham did not hold back his only begotten son. The Hebrews reference is pointed: "He who had received the promises was offering up his *only begotten son*" (italics mine).

Note the wording: *only begotten son*. It is as if the Lord is saying, "Abraham is like me in offering up his only begotten son." In a sense, God was only asking Abraham to be willing to do what he himself would actually do 2,000 years later in Jesus Christ. We sense awe in God's pronouncement regarding the old man's obedience.

---

12   Gal. 3:16.

Abraham's faith had a resurrection quality to it. Likewise, *God is able to resurrect anything we hand over to him.* Can we trust his power and goodness so that ultimately we know Him as our adequate source and supplier?

We may wish we had Abraham's faith and, of course, it is available to those who are willing to die to everything that fails to measure up to God. This kind of life has godlike implications. We are very close to the Father's heart when we withhold nothing from him while remembering, he in turn withheld nothing from us when he gave his Son.

God so loved the world, that He gave His only begotten Son, that whoever believes in Him shall not perish, but have eternal life.[13]

This kind of obedience cannot be contained in the generation in which it occurs. You and I are not being asked to raise the knife against one of our children. But God may still require stringent sacrifice in another area of life, leading to multiple blessings of others. Whatever that area is, like Abraham, we may be called on to die to our expectations.

What is he asking *now*? If you're not sure, start with immediate steps of obedience on the things you *do* know. They can lead to a larger, more comprehensive compliance later.

Is the Lord pointing to something that requires a response? Are you facing the *big one,* as Abraham did? While this tortuous path may require you to climb a terrible mountain, you will not walk alone. With fear and trembling, we can say, "I trust God and leave the results in his hands."

---

13   John 3:16.

DYING TO LIVE APPLICATION

Ask God to prepare you not only for whatever tests he has in store but also for resurrection-like victory and triumph.

QUESTIONS FOR REFLECTION

Abraham and Sarah got Isaac back. Are any of your losses like Isaac if he had actually been sacrificed on the mountain?

If you have a loss that seems irreparable, how do you interact with God about it?

Is your love and worship of God hindered in the face of whatever losses, griefs or wounds you incurred?

⚔ ⚔ ⚔

CHAPTER 3

Elijah: Wanting To Die When the Going Gets Tough

DYING TO LIVE PRINCIPLE
The strongest can become the weakest.

Elijah arises suddenly and unexpectedly in I Kings 17 with a front-page splash.

> Now Elijah the Tishbite, who was one of the settlers of Gilead, said to Ahab, "As the LORD, the God of Israel lives, before whom I stand, surely there shall be neither dew nor rain these years, except by my word."[14]

Was this intrusion before the king by a settler from Gilead like Daniel Boone or Ben Cartwright appearing in Washington, D.C.? Elijah's claim that he stood before the Lord was, on its face, outrageous. The Jews would not even pronounce God's name in its Hebrew form (Yahweh). Was Elijah exhibiting mental instability or delusions of grandeur when he claimed that the dew or rainfall was under his control? The agriculture-based economy depended directly on it.

Amazingly enough, Elijah *was* the man of God he claimed to be. He was the real deal. At this time, pagan religious systems have supplanted the knowledge of the true and living God. The nation of Israel has rejected its future and is

---

14   I Kings 17:1.

slouching toward a tragic national suicide. Elijah is the one God sends holding up a stop sign.

The divine rescue is to be severe. An extended drought occurs as Elijah has prophesied, and the country is brought to its knees. Before it ends, King Ahab himself goes out scrounging for pasture for the royal flocks.

In the midst of the national upheaval, God sends Elijah to camp out by the stream called Cherith, a ravine or wadi east of the Jordan River. There the Lord commandeers ravens to bring him two meals each day, consisting of bread and meat.

From this point on, Elijah's career only becomes more spectacular. Driven from his wadi hideout by the drought, Elijah ends up 80 miles north, on the shores of the Mediterranean in what is today Lebanon. His destination is the home of the widow of Zarephath, who is beginning to starve, along with her son.

Everything Elijah does is dramatic, spectacular, or miraculous. He comes to the widow and demands to be fed while she and her son face certain starvation. Then he performs the miracle of self-replenishing oil and flour to feed them all during the famine. While the woman hosts him in a little room above her quarters, her son dies, so Elijah melodramatically raises him from the dead. Elijah is courageous, available to God, and a survivor.

He marches out from this extended period of quiet retirement to face King Ahab, who has issued an all points bulletin on him. With unmitigated brashness, Elijah suddenly appears and orders the king to bring together the 450 prophets who served Baal. He includes a command to call the 400 Asherah soothsayers stabled by Jezebel. In so doing, Elijah is calling down the fury of both a reprobate king and an evil queen. Elijah is alone in this battle against 850 false prophets, and Ahab is looking for any opportunity to execute him. It will be a battle to the death.

The story unfolds like a classic Hollywood thriller. Elijah once again holds the fate of the nation in his hands. Descriptors fail when you read I Kings 18, one of the most dramatic chapters of the Bible. Here are some easy ones:

- Faithfulness to God,
- courage,
- a lonely encounter against all odds,
- one man against a nation of reprobates, beginning with the king and queen,
- death to the false prophets and life from the eternal God, and
- one of the great "high noon" encounters in human history.

These and any other attempts to capture this episode all fall short, much like the gory attempts of the false prophets to meet Elijah's challenge. They start in the morning and persist through the heat of the day, while the oxen's blood they spill bakes in the sun, drawing innumerable flies while the sun's rays begin to slant from the west. Yet there is not even a spark on their altar to Baal.

Elijah finally steps forward, builds a trench, fills it with water, lays the sacrifice on the refurbished altar, and calls on God.

At the time of the offering of the evening sacrifice, Elijah the prophet came near and said, "O LORD, the God of Abraham, Isaac and Israel, today let it be known that You are God in Israel and that I am Your servant and I have done all these things at Your word. Answer me, O LORD, answer me, that this people may know that You, O LORD, are God, and that You have turned their heart back again." Then the fire of the LORD fell and consumed the burnt offering and the wood and stones and dust, and licked up the water that was in the trench. When all the people saw it, they fell on their faces; and they said, "The LORD, He is God; the LORD, He is God."[15]

The battle to the death is over, decisively. Elijah commands the spiritually revived people to seize the Baal prophets and take them down to Kishon, where the stream is turned red with their blood.

Now in complete control, Elijah commands Ahab to eat and then escape the oncoming deluge. Again, the lonely prophet prayerfully waits with his head between his knees. God once more responds to him with rain–in fact, a storm of blessing— that ends the frightful drought and brings life back to the land.

The scene, however, changes dramatically in the next verses. In a complete reversal, fearless and faithful Elijah is pushed over the emotional edge by Jezebel–the heartless queen of the land.

Now Ahab told Jezebel all that Elijah had done, and how he had killed all the prophets with the sword. Then Jezebel sent a messenger to Elijah, saying, "So may the gods do to me and even more, if I do not make your life as one of them by tomorrow about this time." And he was afraid and arose and ran for his life and came to Beersheba, which belongs to Judah, and left his servant there. But he himself went a day's journey

---

15   I Kings 18:36-39.

into the wilderness, and came and sat down under a juniper tree; and he requested for himself that he might die, and said, "It is enough; now, O Lord, take my life, for I am not better than my fathers." He lay down and slept under a juniper tree; and behold, there was an angel touching him, and he said to him, "Arise, eat." Then he looked and behold, there was at his head a bread cake baked on hot stones, and a jar of water. So he ate and drank and lay down again. The angel of the Lord came again a second time and touched him and said, "Arise, eat, because the journey is too great for you." So he arose and ate and drank, and went in the strength of that food forty days and forty nights to Horeb, the mountain of God.[16]

Immediately following a *Ten Commandments*-type of display of God's absolute authority over a competing religious system, why does Elijah crash and burn? More to the point, why doesn't he stay on the offensive and warn the queen of the danger she faces? After all, a little later he prophesies that the dogs will eat her body.

"Of Jezebel also has the Lord spoken, saying, 'The dogs will eat Jezebel in the district of Jezreel.' The one belonging to Ahab, who dies in the city, the dogs will eat, and the one who dies in the field the birds of heaven will eat."[17]

The fulfillment of this gruesome prophecy comes soon enough.

---

16   I Kings 19:1-8.
17   I Kings 21:23.

29

When Jehu came to Jezreel, Jezebel heard of it, and she painted her eyes and adorned her head and looked out the window. As Jehu entered the gate, she said, "Is it well, Zimri, your master's murderer?" Then he lifted up his face to the window and said, "Who is on my side? Who?" And two or three officials looked down at him. He said, "Throw her down." So they threw her down, and some of her blood was sprinkled on the wall and on the horses, and he trampled her under foot. When he came in, he ate and drank; and he said, "See now to this cursed woman and bury her, for she is a king's daughter." They went to bury her, but they found nothing more of her than the skull and the feet and the palms of her hands. Therefore they returned and told him. And he said, "This is the word of the Lord, which He spoke by His servant Elijah the Tishbite, saying, 'In the property of Jezreel the dogs shall eat the flesh of Jezebel; and the corpse of Jezebel will be as dung on the face of the field in the property of Jezreel, so they cannot say, "This is Jezebel."[18]

Few people possessed the relationship with God that Elijah did. Meanwhile, his most mortal enemy, Jezebel, is sentenced to one of the most horrible and humiliating deaths that could ever befall a royal person. The confrontation between the man of God and this woman of darkness was not, as they say now, on a level playing field. This should have been a slam dunk for Elijah.

Yet after his encounter with the false prophets, Elijah is about to fold when faced with the doomed queen's threats. Jezebel sends him the equivalent of a flame e-mail, saying,

---

18   2 Kings 9:30-37.

"So may the gods do to me and even more, if I do not make your life as the life of one of them by tomorrow about this time." And he was afraid and arose and ran for his life and came to Beersheba, which belongs to Judah, and left his servant there. But he himself went a day's journey into the wilderness, and came and sat down under a juniper tree; and he requested for himself that he might die, and said, "It is enough; now, O LORD, take my life, for I am not better than my fathers."[19]

Faced with this very real threat, a stressed-out Elijah is ready to walk away from his prophetic life. In fact, his greatest wish at the moment is to die. He runs out of gas emotionally, physically and spiritually. He becomes as helpless as a baby as he lies down under the juniper tree.

This pitiful scene reminds me of a haunting song by Twila Paris, "The Warrior Is a Child." It highlights the naked truth that, even in our best warrior mode, we can be broken down to the inner helplessness of a child. After describing the way a mature Christian can feel after winning spiritual battles in life, the lyrics of the song shift to the inner life. Anyone who has survived a battle knows that winning comes with a price, sometimes at great personal cost. Back home people congratulate you and give hearty pats on the back for a job well done. But there's something uncomfortable about all this praise. Kind words like "you're amazing" and "strong" seem out of sync with what the warrior realizes after the party's over. Most people can't see what's really going on inside us. And then the song discloses the truth:

---

19   I Kings 19:2b-4.

I drop my sword and cry for just a while
'Cause deep inside this armor
The warrior is a child

Have you ever seen a child under stress simply "lose it"? Perhaps he forgot his homework, or was the butt of a cutting remark on the playground, or fell off his bike. Instantly the smile disappears under a torrent of tears, the child's confident self-sufficiency drowned in an ocean of helplessness. I see the same thing happening as Elijah collapses after his strenuous day in the sun.

At his strongest, the mighty Elijah was just one crisis away from becoming a blubbering, helpless infant, from dying to his own sufficiency. And so are we all.

O that we Christian leaders would die Elijah's death *before* our broken lives and reputations make headlines! A Christian leader, pastor, missionary or prophetic voice may tower above his or her contemporaries. It makes no difference who we are or what we have done—we are never far from being a temporary or permanent casualty.

One incident stands out. A leader enjoyed a spectacular ministry career. This man pastored a large church. His books were read by thousands. He seemed to be a headliner at every major conference. The day I heard him speak, he observed that sexual temptation was not a problem for him.

A few months later, he was named president of a major Christian organization. But before he took office, he admitted to an affair! Why? It was an Elijah episode! It wasn't the kind of lust that troubles many men, whose eyes wander regularly where they should not. It was a stress-based lapse like Elijah's. In this man's great weariness and fatigue, the gentle and comforting possibility of a female relationship became his juniper tree . . . and he lay down there.

Christian leader–whoever or wherever you are, however important or powerful you may be, no matter how many are depending on you, and no matter if you are bigger than life– you are not invincible. You can find yourself under a juniper tree in a far more compromised position than was Elijah.

Before that happens, pray something like this:

"The warrior is a child. Lord, I am not big enough, strong enough or tough enough to fight every battle to the end without your protective care. Lord, feed me Elijah's angel food or better yet, feed me the bread of heaven and hold me up when I am close to collapse. Help me to go in your strength, as Elijah did, for 40 days or 40 months or 40 years. Help me to stand on Mount Horeb, as he did, and hear your gentle voice. Help me when it is time to go and find my Elisha, to put a mantle of leadership on him and fade off the scene just like Elijah did!" (2 Kings 2)

Get serious, before the crisis comes. Sit under your juniper tree for a while. Confess your weakness and dependence. Reflect on how close you are to walking away from your honored position and wishing to die. Only then will you be prepared to get up and serve with humility and grace. Then you can serve the eternal God in *his* strength until he calls you to give your mantle to the next freshly anointed one, who will follow your model and serve faithfully, as you did.

DYING TO LIVE APPLICATION

Be prepared to receive God's resources when yours are gone.

QUESTIONS FOR REFLECTION

What is the closest you have come to an Elijah-like collapse?

How do you know when you are moving to a danger zone where you are vulnerable to a crash?

How indispensable are you? Are you okay with an Elisha eventually taking the baton you have been carrying? (2 Kings 2)

✠ ✠ ✠

CHAPTER 4

Paul (2 Corinthians): When an Apostle Despaired

DYING TO LIVE PRINCIPLE
Transformation often trails trauma.

When we moved from Virginia to Chicago, survival as a parachurch chaplain was difficult, to say the least. Sometimes our existence was a little desperate. A long commute, a full day as a chaplain, another job until midnight, constant financial shortfalls, finding adequate provision for our family, and other non-negotiable responsibilities helped generate numbing stress. Life was too dark, uncertain, and full of tension to get a rational start to the day.

When I awakened during the night, I would spiral into an abyss of uncontrollable anxiety. Over time I learned that I could not afford the luxury of thinking during these long night watches, because nothing good ever came of it. So I refused to think until I gained perspective from my morning Bible reading.

Other times, I have been even less rational. One morning in my office, my drooping spirits were inexplicably lifting. My pessimistic response to this unexpected development, however, shocked even my depressed mind.

"Light shining through the clouds of my life is not helpful right now," I thought. "It disrupts the rhythm to which I am accustomed. It is easier to live in my darkness than cope with a day or so of feeling better and then having to adjust back the next day to my life's standard cheerlessness. I don't want a bright day today and then have to drop back into a cloud bank tomorrow. At least I am finding an even keel when everything seems so dismal. Bouncing up one day and falling off the cliff the next doesn't help much. I can do without this rebound."

So I can identify, at least a little bit, with the high stress the Apostle Paul endured. He easily could have lost his life. He wrestled with despair, deep discouragement, and perhaps depression—and he wasn't ashamed to say so.

> For we do not want you to be unaware, brethren, of our affliction which came to us in Asia, that we were burdened excessively, beyond our strength, so that we despaired even of life; indeed, we had the sentence of death within ourselves so that we would not trust in ourselves, but in God who raises the dead.[20]

How much can we find out about this dark period of his life? What did Paul want the Corinthian Christians to gain from his experience? And how does all this relate to our theme, dying to live?

In this account from 2 Corinthians, Paul does not provide details about his missionary team's hardships in Asia, but I will highlight two corroborating episodes from the Book of Acts that will allow us to identify with this grim period.

The first gives a sense of movement. The apostle is pushing on, regardless of whether he needs rest, healing, and restoration of soul. The team is traveling relentlessly. In quick succession, it visits Seleucia, Cyprus, Salamis and Paphos (Acts 13:4-6). Perga in Pamphylia and Pisidian Antioch follow (Acts 13:13-14). Paul and company move on to Lycaonia, Lystra, Derbe, Pisidia,

---

20   2 Corinthians 1:8-9.

Pamphlia, Attalia and back to Antioch on the rim of Asia Minor in northern Syria (Acts 14:6, 24-26).

They keep driving on, with minimal care for their bodies and general well being. Then it really gets tough.

But Jews came from Antioch and Iconium, and having won over the crowds, they stoned Paul and dragged him out of the city, supposing him to be dead. But while the disciples stood around him, he got up and entered the city. The next day he went away with Barnabas to Derbe. After they had preached the gospel to that city and had made many disciples, they returned to Lystra and to Iconium and to Antioch.[21]

I can hardly believe this heartbreaking account – stoned and taken for dead one day, getting up and going back into the city, pushing on to Derbe and other cities of the ancient world. Today's overworked and overstressed pastors have nothing on Paul.

It takes little imagination to link this period in Asia Minor with the apostle's afflictions, burdens, and despair. There is no letup as he responds immediately to the Macedonian call and sails across the Aegean for what, perhaps unbeknown to him, turns out to be one of the most significant points of his ministry.

I have knelt for prayer by the stream in Philippi, where Lydia became the first European convert and was baptized with other members of her household. The modern "Lydia's Church," adjacent to this site, celebrates the advent of the gospel to Europe. Philippi was a key city on the eastern end of the

---

21   Acts 14:19-21.

Egnatian Way–a thoroughfare for merchants and soldiers traveling between the eastern part of the empire and Rome.

Even at this high point, troubles continue to dog Paul's trail. His wounded body and soul remain under severe assault.

> The crowd rose up together against them, and the chief magistrates tore their robes off them and proceeded to order them to be beaten with rods. When they had struck them with many blows, they threw them into prison, commanding the jailer to guard them securely; and he, having received such a command, threw them into the inner prison and fastened their feet in the stocks. But about midnight Paul and Silas were praying and singing hymns of praise to God, and the prisoners were listening to them.[22]

It would be easy to wonder why God allowed all this suffering when Paul and Silas were doing no more than following their divinely sourced orders. For Paul to be beaten with rods after his recent stoning is almost inconceivable. However, we cannot let our emotions cloud our view of the bigger picture. At street level, all we can see is chaos and pain. From the air, however, we see God sovereignly and strategically opening doors for the advance of his kingdom. The Bible is clear that we must do the same in our own lives—look at our individual circumstances in light of larger kingdom priorities. While Paul faced a lamentable struggle, he was an instrument of God to help bring about a great moment in the history of the church.

The gospel had not yet penetrated Europe. The future of a continent and even more hangs in the balance. There is a sense in which even the United States will eventually be impacted in

---

22   Acts 16:22-25.

Philippi, along a stream where today many pilgrims and tourists come every year. The gospel has begun its march westward in Europe. It will continue to Rome and then northwest to England and to the wild frontier of Ireland, where it will morph into the Celtic church.

Listen again as the apostle describes the cost it demanded personally.

> We were burdened excessively, beyond our strength, so that we despaired even of life; indeed, we had the sentence of death within ourselves so that we would not trust in ourselves, but in God who raises the dead.[23]

Paul's painful account is the underside of an extremely significant juncture of church history. Our lives, though perhaps played out on a smaller stage, also contain pivotal moments. And, like Paul, we often face a high price for the many life-changing experiences that come our way and bring blessings to us and those in our circle. Some victories, usually the greatest ones, cannot be purchased for experiential pennies.

Ivan Pavlov, the Russian physiologist, conducted his now famous experiments on dogs in the early 20th century. His laboratories were situated along a river in Russia. When flood waters rose at one point, the dogs had to be rescued. In a section for vicious canines with psychotic personalities where the water was not too deep, cages were opened and the dogs were allowed to swim out. In another section where the waters had risen to the tops of the cages, the dogs were submerged and had to come out *under water*. This experience, which was alien to anything they had experienced previously, radically

---

23   2 Cor. 1:8-9.

changed them—their viciousness disappeared. The other dogs, however, experienced no change.

What had happened? In retrospect, the answer is simple—simple, that is, if you don't have to go through it! The principle is that some deeply entrenched reality, defect, shortcoming or *mode of living* can be changed through a suffocating, life-threatening experience. It happened with those dogs, and it can happen with us.

In other words, what is native to your life, what is part of the fabric of your life, what is formatted into your personality, *can be changed.* Some event or circumstance floods into our lives and drowns our normal coping capability. It is here that we either drown emotionally or spiritually or discover resurrection life in Christ becoming activated in that stunted, distorted area of life.

Paul was referring to this kind of life-changing experience in his compressed comments to the Corinthians. He says essentially that "my helpless, despairing, depressing, desperate and dismal circumstances in Asia became my springboard to a new level of living, a spiritual resurrection within, in which the life of God immersed my human existence at a level I never experienced before."

A modern manufacturing process reminds me of what happens in this kind of extreme life development. It is called extrusion. In extrusion, heat, pressure and cooling combine to produce a semi-liquid substance that is forced through a die and is afterward hardened into a new form. Doesn't this relate to what God is doing in us in the hard episodes of life? Under the heat and pressure of these circumstances, something new is formatted and shaped within. While analogous to extrusion it is even more mysterious and miraculous. And . . . this new form allows us to resemble Christ more closely than ever before.

When speaking to business leaders–company owners, presidents and entrepreneurs—it is hard to convey this kind of hard truth in the brief time we have together. I don't want to appear cavalier or sound so "spiritual" that my approach seems grossly negligent. There is no way I can breezily say, "You may lose your company with millions of dollars in investments, the place where dozens of employees make a living for their families, be forced to forfeit what took more than a generation to build and walk out with nothing so your family is left to face what they could not imagine before you lost it all. But it's going to be OK if you just walk with the Lord." How much credibility would I have after delivering this kind of super-spiritual message?

In our sessions together, one of the things I focus on is how the company and its leader can survive and thrive, rather than nosedive into the rubble of business failures. That kind of counsel is expected, and it is perfectly fine. There is nothing inherently good about failure, and it is natural to try to avoid it. This kind of planning evidences how God has made us in his image as builders and sustainers, attempting to keep chaos at bay. But every chapter in this book opens up a vista through which we can see that God's plan for our lives is often beyond anything we can own, operate or lead. We are not allowed to limit ourselves to what is typical. Sometimes God calls us to move beyond normal.

When Paul was beaten badly and jailed along with his ministry partner, Silas, why couldn't he say to himself, "This is not working, so I must have been on a wrong frequency"? Facing your own struggles, have you ever had a similar monologue? Who *hasn't*? But personal costs are on only one side of the ledger. What about the assets?

In Paul's case, we have some hard numbers. Lydia was converted and baptized along with her household. The Philippian jailer was converted, and his household professed faith as well. Very soon these believers and others are referred to as a church. The epistle they later received from the apostle while he was under house arrest in Rome indicates that they were among the most vibrant church groups in the ancient world.

If you were to sit by the river side for a morning with Lydia's Church in the background, as I have, and thought about the results of the apostle's ministry during this life phase, what conclusions might you draw? Imagine a great stadium, like the Big House at the University of Michigan that seats more than 100,000 people, on this site. The river Strymon flows right through it, as it did in Philippi when it formed part of the boundary of northern Macedonia. Lydia's Church would be enclosed by this huge stadium.

Who else might be in this gigantic arena? Let's suppose people are selected like those on *American Idol* or another TV talent show. They are selected because they stand out from their peers in talent, performance ability, or accomplishments. Each person in this mammoth stadium is outstanding for at least one reason. Yet each one represents many others who are similar in accomplishment or character. This people-filled stadium represents millions more who are not there.

Suppose it is possible to project on huge screens the scene in which the convert Lydia and her household are baptized in the river Strymon. Imagine the stadium falling silent, the people transfixed, as Paul speaks quietly and powerfully to

Lydia. When she decides to belong to Christ in the midst of her pagan environment in this rough, Romanized town, imagine the cheer that rocks the stadium. It can be heard all the way to the ruins of ancient Philippi.

Each spectator can trace his or her spiritual lineage to Lydia, the Philippian church and the other Macedonian churches from which the gospel radiated to the Roman Empire and beyond. The good news had broken loose from Asia and was beginning its relentless march west, eventually jumping the Atlantic to North America and other parts of the world.

These freshly formed European churches were aggressive. Paul speaks to the Thessalonians that

> You became an example to all the believers in Macedonia and in Achaia. For the word of the Lord has sounded forth from you, not only in Macedonia and Achaia, but also in every place your faith toward God has gone forth, so that we have no need to say anything.[24]

This vigor is still coursing through the spiritual veins of mighty missionary movements from the 19th century through today. Countless others reached by them—new believers in Asia, Africa, and Latin America—over the centuries have grasped the gospel baton, lived, spent their lives and died as servants of the Most High. They too can trace their roots back to this scene.

When I think of the astounding, unimaginable and immeasurable development of Christianity in the West, I am certain about something else: I wouldn't make the 100,000 cut to sit in the stadium, and, with all due respect, I doubt if you would

---

24   1 Thess. 1:7-8.

either! There are just too many amazing followers of Christ: founders of great movements; thousands of martyrs; theologians; statesmen; composers; common people such as Brother Lawrence, who reached very high levels of spiritual development; authors and reformers who changed the course of history; founders of universities, hospitals and other institutions that mirror the mercy of God. We might not qualify to sit beside these giants, but perhaps we could sell hot dogs at the concession stand!

Yet you and I have no right to stand in the place of God and say, "My life is of little consequence." Aren't there single moms, former homosexuals, alcoholics, and addicts who are faithfully following God's call, whatever it is? If Rahab, the harlot from 3,000 years ago, remains a hero worthy of emulation, why not you? Are you running a multimillion-dollar company as a follower of Christ? Are you occupying a high office under the higher authority and call of Christ? Or are you scrubbing toilets at a summer camp? If we are doing what God wants us to do, let God determine our importance and reward.

Are you enduring a dying, impossible time, as Paul did in Asia? If so, hang on! Pray! Would one of the following requests fit the state of your heart?

- "Lord, have mercy on me as I don't think I've got it in me to persevere as the apostle did. Help me to be faithful when my way is dark, as his was."
- "Lord, I don't think I can make it any further–help! As I stand on the brink of losing everything, help me see beyond my short-sightedness."
- "Lord, even if I can handle what I am facing, I'm not sure I can stand what it might do to those I love. Help me

yield to the bigness of your plan and get beyond what I am seeing as disaster at this time."

- "Lying here in this hospital bed and facing continual pain day after day, when I thought I was going to be a wife and mother, has drowned me in a pool of hopelessness. Lord, I understand that you are the sufficient answer to what seems to be pure darkness with no good solution. Just help me get through what I have no resources to endure and navigate. Lord . . . !"

Should you find yourself in such desperate circumstances, may you experience the spiritual resurrection the Lord offers. When you do, perhaps you will encourage other hurting people with your story while you leave the ultimate results in his hands.

DYING TO LIVE APPLICATION

Endure your darkness; experience what you must and become . . . !

QUESTIONS FOR REFLECTION

Do you recall a time in your life when you were deeply discouraged or despairing? How would you describe it?

Are you still grieved or are you okay with it now? Why?

Are you able now to stand with or relate to others in a dark season of their lives in a more meaningful way?

CHAPTER 5

X X X

Jacob: Peniel–Mayday . . . Mayday . . . Mayday

DYING TO LIVE PRINCIPLE
*Personal desperation and darkness can
become your doorway to nobility.*

Chesley Sullenberger once said that few pilots ever have to endure an *incident* in their flying careers. But on January 15, 2009, Capt. Sullenberger and his co-pilot, Jeffrey Skiles, suddenly faced one. Three minutes after takeoff, they were on a routine climb over New York City on US Airways Flight 1549 when a bird strike took out both engines. Learning that they couldn't safely make it to an airfield, Sullenberger glided the Airbus 320 and its 155 occupants over the Hudson River, where he ditched the aircraft, saving all aboard. This *mayday* experience was extreme–we know of no other water landing of a commercial jet without a single loss of life.

To avoid any doubt or confusion the international distress message is always given as *mayday … mayday … mayday*. It derives from the French, *venez m'aider*, which means, "Come help me."

Horrendous crises, like US Airways Flight 1549, can barge into our lives without notice. They level the playing field of humanity, whether we are at the bottom, the top, or somewhere in between. They create circumstances that change our lives forever. The biblical patriarch Jacob had to pray *mayday* at Peniel, because there was no human being who could help him against his brother, Esau. Jacob's *mayday* cry was directed to God and God alone. But first he had to undergo some long, painful decades of preparation.

Jacob had already endured 20 grueling years in his father-in-law's house after running for his life from Esau. He served seven years for the love of his life, Rachel. After Leah was substituted, he served another seven for Rachel.[25]

Jacob, whose name means "holder of the heel" or "supplanter," took both Esau's birthright and blessing with the eventual result that he fled to Paddam-Aran (modern day Syria) to save his life. There he drove a bargain with Laban and spent the next several years building his own herds and flocks. Even with Laban attempting to cheat him at every turn, God protected and prospered Jacob. Eventually he took his now large family and agribusiness on hoofs and disappeared, heading southwest, back toward Canaan.

The final challenge was to let Esau know he was coming back. As a wealthy and influential man, with 20 years behind them both, Jacob could only assume they could patch things up enough to live separately in a very large area. They wouldn't even be in the same country, as Esau lived in today's Jordan, east of Israel.

As Jacob approaches his homeland, he sends messengers to make contact with Esau. The report comes back that Esau is returning with a band of 400 men. This meeting would be like 400 green berets overrunning a family picnic. Jacob's family, servants and animals are completely vulnerable. Jacob is rightly terrified at the news.

---

25 Substantial sections of this chapter are taken from my book *Beyond Leadership to Destiny–Jacob's Lifetime Journey with God* in the chapter entitled, "Peniel–Crisis Transformation."

Apparently, according to Genesis 32, Jacob had already forgotten a huge sign of God's protection. Just before he learned that Esau and 400 men are heading his way, the angels of God actually met Jacob. He even recognized them, exclaiming, "This is God's host!" Of course, he had seen angels at Bethel years earlier. Just as he had done at Bethel, Jacob immediately consecrated the place with a name, Mahanaim, a Hebrew term meaning "two camps," in reference to his own entourage or perhaps to the angels appearing in two divisions.

But with a rendezvous with Esau dead ahead, the significance of God's angels seems now to be lost on Jacob. He fails to realize that God's army of angels could make Esau's 400 men of no more consequence than a few harmless flies.

After hearing of Esau's company, "Jacob [is] greatly afraid and distressed." He prays a desperate plea, "O God of my father Abraham and God of my father Isaac." Jacob prays, not out of his own experience, but merely with an inherited reality of God from his father and grandfather: "Deliver me, I pray, from the hand of my brother, from the hand of Esau; for I fear him, that he will come and attack me and the mothers with the children." He chokes out his confession of fear for himself and his family. This kind of honesty is sometimes difficult for men.[26]

Before Jacob asks God to remember that he is the One who told Jacob to return home, the heel-grabber makes a startling confession: "I am unworthy of all the lovingkindness and of all the faithfulness which You have shown to Your servant; for with my staff only I crossed this Jordan, and now I have become two companies."[27]

---

26   See Gen 32:7-11.

27   Gen. 32:10.

Think about it. If you were in the worst crisis you ever faced, would you tell God first that you didn't deserve his intervention? In the face of death, Jacob gives evidence that he has grown significantly since Bethel, when he asked God for contractual guarantees before he would agree to be his servant.

So Jacob begs God for mercy and kindness. And he is on solid ground, because God has already promised to bless Jacob with descendents who would be as numerous as the sands on the seashore. Jacob's fate and that of every member of his family, along with his ambitions, plans and possessions, were all out of his hands. In his prayer he transfers them to God.

Jacob prays as if his life and the lives of his family depend on God. But he is still a cunning strategist who comes up with a plan to appease Esau. And so he offers his brother a generous gift (or bribe—it doesn't really matter to Jacob as long as Esau is happy) of 550 head of livestock. They were enough to make a person instantly wealthy. He hopes the present will encourage his brother to forget about the past.

Jacob's life to this point reminds me of an ancient truth about metallurgy. A blacksmith heats a piece of metal until it is red hot. Then he strikes an insignificant blow with a small hammer. This nicking marks the spot where the heavy sledge will smash the metal to mold it to its final shape. God had brought Jacob to Bethel and marked his life for years of formation. He had been in the fire for 20 years and said as much.[28] Now he is on the anvil to receive the molding blow, from which he will be permanently injured, limping away with a new name and ultimately a new identity.

His time "alone with the Alone," (to borrow a phrase from Catholic mysticism), occurs along the banks of the Jabbok

---

28   Gen. 31:40-41.

River. The words of Brother Roger of Taize are apt: "In every one lies a zone of solitude that no human intimacy can fill; and there God encounters us."[29]

After sending his wives and children across, Jacob *is* alone, suspended between the only two worlds he knows. The door to Laban's house is shut forever. The only other place for Jacob is the land to which he has been commanded to return. Yet Esau stands in the way. As he weighs his predicament, something freezes Jacob's attention, a dim shadow of a figure. Is it Esau the aggressor? The thought probably makes him sick. He might not even live to the next day! He reacts with the pent-up fury, fear or frenzy that can make one man a temporary match for several. There is nothing left to do but attack the assailant. And attack is what Jacob does.

As the wrestling match continues through the night, a stark reality forces its way into Jacob's traumatized senses: "It's not Esau and it's not one of his men. I don't know who it is, but he is not my enemy." Imperceptibly, he begins to understand that his opponent has come primarily as a solution, and only secondarily as a wrestler. Jacob realizes that he does not have to fight this shadowy aggressor, but he refuses to give up the fight without some answers.

As the morning light begins to dawn, the unknown contestant touches Jacob's hip joint and cripples him for life. Jacob's injury became so sacred to successive generations of Jews that they refuse to eat the meat from this part of an animal.[30]

Now Jacob is both exhausted and injured. He can no longer stand or walk without a limp, but he can still cling. When

---

29   Quoted in Charles Haley, *Beyond Leadership to Destiny – Jacob's Lifetime Journey with God: Spiritual Formation for Third Millennium Leaders* (Wheaton: Life Serve Ltd., 2005), 133.

30   Gen. 32:32.

his opponent demands, "Let me go, for the dawn is breaking," Jacob's response is simple and desperate: "I will not let you go unless you bless me."[31] Here is a man of God contending for the blessing of God. And Jacob's desperate demand is granted![32]

However, the blessing is preceded by an unexpected question: "What is your name?" And Jacob tells him.[33] Jacob's life is pictured in his name, and in his answer: "I am a heel grabber!" is the idea implicit in his name. But things are about to change. The Wrestler answers, "Your name shall no longer be Jacob, but Israel. You have become a prince, a prevailer, one who has power with God and with men."

At this startling announcement, Jacob asks a question that is really unnecessary, "Please tell me Your name," only to be asked another question, "Why do you ask My name?" The One who names must be greater than the one who is named. Does the mystery Wrestler have sufficient authority to change Jacob's name and identity? Of course! Jacob names the place Peniel, "Face of God," and receives the blessing of the divine Wrestler.

Some people find the question, "What is your name?" terrifying because it seeks an identity. Too often the answer is, "I could never tell you who I am. I don't know who I am, or I can't even admit who I am to myself. I look successful, but I'm messed up. I would trade my home, my portfolio, my antique collection or whatever else I value to stop what I am doing but keep hidden. I'll probably never get straightened out."

The forced solitude and struggle at Peniel can be a model for us. Robert Mulholland captures it well.

31 Gen. 32:26.
32 Gen. 32:29.
33 Gen. 32:27.

This is what solitude is: in the silence of releasing control of our relationship with God to God, coming face to face with the kind of person we are in the depths of our being; seeing the depths of our grasping manipulative, self-indulgent behavior; facing the brokenness, the darkness, the uncleanness that is within; acknowledging our bondages, our false securities, our posturing facades; and naming ourselves to God as this kind of person ... In silence we let go our manipulative control. In solitude we face up to what we are in the depths of our being. Prayer then becomes the offering of who we are to God: the giving of that broken, unclean, grasping, manipulative self to God for the work of God's grace in our lives.[34]

At Peniel, we face ourselves, as Jacob did. Jacob answered, "I am Jacob. I am a supplanter, a cheater, a heel-grabber." At Peniel, we hear our name, when it is forced out of us in our desperately dark hour. We confess who we are, no matter how bad it looks and feels. The awesome reality is that at these times God enters our broken lives to identify what *he* sees us to be.[35] And his pronouncement assures the result. When he says, "It is *Israel*, Prince with God," then *Israel* it really is.

Jacob contended with the Lord to become something he could never be on his own . . . a prince with God. The Old Testament prophet Hosea summarizes the metamorphosis in this way: "In the womb he took his brother by the heel, and in his maturity he contended with God. Yes, he wrestled with the angel and prevailed; he wept and sought His favor."[36]

---

34   M. Robert Mulholland Jr, *Invitation to a Journey: A Road Map for Spiritual Formation* (Downers Grove IL: InterVarsity Press, 1993), 140.

35   2 Cor. 5:17.

36   Hos. 12:3-4.

We see here a mysterious pattern of grabbing in Jacob's life. It began with cleverness and deceit, but it culminated at Peniel, where he contended with God and prevailed. Four verbs are used in the concluding sentence: *wrestled, prevailed, wept,* and *sought.*

In the previous two verses, Hosea has noted that the people are pursuing everything but God, resulting in impending national disaster. Now, he calls them to be like Jacob, wrestling with God. They are to weep at midnight while they hang onto the Lord, when death may come the next day. Hosea tells the people, who are injured and brokenhearted, to seek God. Hosea promises the people that they will prevail with God and he will bless them.

I used to test-drive tractors. One night the dreaded order came: "You're on the torture track tonight!" On the torture track, months of testing were compressed into hours to get a production model tractor ready for use around the world. The tractor I was assigned had more than 4,000 pounds of extra weight attached to the front axle, the equivalent of two compact cars. It had to be driven over large ridges or speed bumps for the entire shift.

So when I began my shift, I did what I could to soften the beating my body was sure to take—unfortunately, to very little effect. I jammed my feet across the windshield crossbar to prevent back injury and instead was thrown into the ceiling. Nothing I did helped, and the torture track was as bad as everyone predicted it would be.

Soon after my shift, we learned that one of our tractors was being shipped to Nebraska to become a production model for use around the world. The torture track, where equipment groaned or screamed all night long, was finished. The tractor our firm finally approved was prepared to perform at the highest levels–*ready for use around the world.*

That's what happened to Jacob at Peniel–he became a production model! He spent 20 years on the test track with Uncle Laban and endured a stint on the torture track at Peniel. At sunrise the next day he limped out with his model designation, *Prince with God*. That's what God is doing at our Peniels–making us production models to stand the test of time and beyond. It is just as Kenneth Caraway once wrote, "There is no box . . . but that the sides can be flattened out and the top blown off to make a dance floor on which to celebrate."[37]

Peniel is not primarily a package but a principle. Jacob's encounter was limited to a few square yards along a small river flowing from the eastern frontier in Gilead to the Jordan. Time limitations made it an experience of twelve hours or less.[38]

Your Peniel may extend halfway around the world, through burning days and anguished months. The predetermined end is the same. In the darkness of a major life crisis, God will lead you to wrestle from him the blessing of a lifetime. In these great, suffocating experiences, the ugly things so twisted into the fabric of our lives, without any possibility of being changed, can and will be changed. This is the Peniel Principle.

Before Peniel, Jacob had been delivered from his bruising, stressful 20-year stint in Syria with Laban, who had continually maligned and mistreated him. There was no way God would pile even more on him, right?

Perhaps you have gone on well with God and have finally achieved most of your dreams. You understand that the

---

37 Quoted in Haley, *Beyond Leadership to Destiny*, 134.
38 Gen. 32:22, 24.

company you have built, the family you have raised, the financial stability you have obtained, or the level of fulfillment you have experienced is a gift from God—and you hold it tightly. There is no way that what you laboriously built with God's help, whether a lot or a little, would be threatened with disaster ... right?

Would you dare to cross the Jabbok and sit in the blackest of darkness, utterly alone? If you have walked into the darkness of Peniel, stay a little longer. The result will not be darkness, a nihilistic outcome or a broken, empty life in which nothing that is lost is ever replaced. This is, after all, *pheni* (face) *el* (God). This is Peniel where, yes, everything in your space-time world will potentially be gone forever. But this terrible night will end for you with the face of God, the Person of God, the wonder of God, the reality of God and the fullness of God. This Face will eclipse everything that disappeared into the swirling night mists.

Some time ago, I realized that I too had gained a limp that I would never outgrow–a grief that was too deep to fully explain. Slowly, I began to embrace this life reality as a special gift tailored just for me. I recognized It as a requirement and a provision to get where I need to go and become who I am called to be.

Strangely enough, the depth of this inner condition is more than matched by a heightened sense of joy, meaning and character development. Peniel for me became an opportunity to discover a hidden part of the plan God has for my life. Jacob began the night terrified of Esau and left in triumph as Israel, Prince with God. He prevailed in an experience he would have avoided at all costs if it had been up to him. We may be called upon to do the same!

If we are called to undergo a personal Peniel, we will also limp out of this Jabbok wadi, this hidden streambed, with a knowledge and reality of God so deeply inscribed on our being that it will forever distinguish our lives. Jacob had to die in one night and then limp the rest of his life to reach the high calling of God. Nothing less than the stature of *Prince with God* would do. Are you likewise coming to grips with your own Peniel Principle? Living through a turning point with God drives the change process, as it has for countless others before you.

A certain renown settles on the person who wrestles with God and survives the dark night. Somehow, at some level, transformation occurs deep within. Survivors of Peniel know God thereafter at a deeper level. Their spiritual knowledge becomes branded into the sinew of their souls.

No one wants to risk everything during a lonely, dark night. I certainly don't. Avoid Peniel if you can. Endure it if you must. But if you face God over the Jabbok, expect to discover your own special renown.

DYING TO LIVE APPLICATION

Trust God for the potential greatness that can emerge from your brokenness and permanent "limp."

QUESTIONS FOR REFLECTION

What makes a Peniel experience so traumatic? Have you or another person with whom you are close undergone a period or incident like this?

Even though you would avoid a Peniel-type occurrence for yourself or anyone you love, why might you accept it in the end?

What kind of life development would you want if this kind of happening was forced into your life?

CHAPTER 6

ꖌ ꖌ ꖌ

The Prodigal: Dying to Become a Father

DYING TO LIVE PRINCIPLE
Accept the Father's love and share it freely.

Which artist speaks to you? Is it your own child, now much older, whose crude, decades-old crayon drawing communicates a simple, artless love that warms your heart every time you retrieve it from the basement? Or were you held captive before a painting in an art museum and now retain its every detail in your memory?

A work in the famous Art Institute of Chicago is burned indelibly into my brain cells. On one visit, the man standing next to me had come all the way from Europe to see it. I don't need it in front of me to feel its uncanny power. Job's head is tilted toward God–his noble face picturing patient suffering and inner strength. The striking lines of his strong, bronzed body, clothed in rags, somehow communicate Job's developed character and godliness. This piece calls my heart to God in a compelling manner each time I stand in front of it.

I have lived with another painting, a famous one, though I have never stood before it. Its impact was driven home through the eyes of another. Fifteen years ago, one of our children gave me a book that he felt my soul needed. The author, Henri Nouwen, a Dutch Trappist monk, is one of the few Roman Catholic authors as widely read by Protestants as by Catholics.

Nouwen's sometimes anguished openness out of a distressed life demands a hearing across the barriers that normally separate us. For me, this volume, *The Return of the Prodigal Son*,[39] is one of the towering works of the last half of the 20th century. Today my copy is yellowed and features multiple markings. Henri Nouwen's story has gripped me from the first. Leaving a Harvard professorship and the prestige that accompanied it, Nouwen eventually fled to a L'Arche community in Trosly, France. Nouwen was dangerously depleted and vulnerable after an exhausting ministry schedule across the United States. There he chanced to see a reproduction of Rembrandt's *Prodigal Son* and was transfixed.

"The tender embrace of father and son expressed everything I desired at that moment," Nouwen writes. "I was, indeed, the son exhausted from long travels; I wanted to be embraced; I was looking for a home where I could feel safe. The son-come-home was all I was and all that I wanted to be... It had brought me into touch with something within me that lies far beyond the ups and downs of a busy life, something that represents the ongoing yearning of the human spirit, the yearning for a final return, an unambiguous sense of safety, a lasting home... It was the hands–the old man's hands–as they touched the boy's shoulders that reached me in a place where I had never been reached before."[40] Nouwen was just beginning his journey with Rembrandt's *Prodigal Son*.

During the next couple of years, Nouwen's soul remained gripped by this great painting, which was acquired in 1776 by Catherine the Great for the Hermitage in Saint Petersburg, where

---

39   Henri Nouwen, *The Return of the Prodigal Son: A Story of Homecoming* (New York: Image Books/Doubleday, 1994).

40   Nouwen, *Return of the Prodigal Son*, 4, 5.

Rembrandt's *Prodigal Son* (iStock photography)

it remains on display. On an unexpected trip, Nouwen ended up in the Russian city, and his first thought was how to see it.

However, he lost hope of spending significant time with *Prodigal Son* when he saw a line of people a mile long waiting to get into the Hermitage. But Nouwen was able to make arrangements with someone who had connections and so entered a side door, far from the throngs. He spent parts of two days sitting in front of the magnificent painting, measuring six by eight feet. The work exceeded his expectations.

Nouwen's book culminates with a chapter on the father. Years later, I was driven there because a near and dear relationship had turned into darkness and separation. I couldn't get rid of the hurt–my weak defense mechanisms in this fragile area were easily penetrated. Because the pain remained deep within, its toxicity was amplified by rage, resentment and rejection–the very opposite of what is portrayed in the chapter on the father. I was failing in this precious and most basic relationship and would do so for years.

In the version of *The Return of the Prodigal Son* that I possess, the painting takes up the cover, and another copy folds out so the reader can refer to it at any time. Nouwen says, "Though I am both the younger son and the elder son, I am not to remain there, but to become the Father. No father or mother ever became father or mother without having been son or daughter, but every son and daughter has to consciously choose to step beyond their childhood and became father and mother for others. It is a hard and lonely step to take."[41]

After too many lost opportunities, the message was beginning to get through. For the next several years, I was haunted by this painting through Nouwen, who wrote, "Indeed, as son and heir I am to become successor. I am destined to step into my Father's place and offer to others the same compassion that he has offered me."[42] I can't read these words even now without deep grief, a desire to repent forever, and a determination to be father at a genuine level. Nouwen says it for me: "I have to dare to stretch out my own hands in blessing and to receive with ultimate compassion my children, regardless of how they feel or think about me."[43]

"Regardless of how they feel or think about me." That conviction was approaching the message coming home to me, as

41 Ibid., 121.
42 Ibid., 123.
43 Ibid., 124.

well. My reaction, choice or commitment to someone does not depend on how the beloved person is or is not responding to me. After all, doesn't God love us because of who *he* is instead of who we are?

This kind of "spiritual fatherhood," Nouwen writes, "has nothing to do with power or control. It is a fatherhood of compassion."[44] Nouwen says that compassionate fatherhood involves grief, forgiveness and generosity. "Grief asks me to allow the sins of the world–my own included–to pierce my heart and make me shed tears. . . Grief allows me to see beyond my wall and realize the immense suffering that results from human lostness."[45]

Spiritual fatherhood puts the other person first—at great personal cost. Nouwen writes, "As the Father, I have to dare to carry the responsibility of a spiritually adult person and dare to trust that the real joy and real fulfillment can only come from welcoming home those who have been hurt and wounded on their life's journey, and loving them with a love that neither asks nor expects anything in return. There is a dreadful emptiness in this spiritual fatherhood. . . that sacred emptiness of non-demanding love."[46]

Yes, Nouwen acknowledges the blessings of being in a loving community, but he says such encouragement is "a way station on the road to a much more lonely destination: the loneliness of the Father, the loneliness of God, the ultimate loneliness of compassion. A father who only blesses in endless compassion, asking no questions, always giving and forgiving,

---

44   Ibid., 127.
45   Ibid., 128.
46   Ibid., 132-133.

never expecting anything in return." Of this, Nouwen says the "the pains are too obvious, the joys too hidden."[47]

We cannot sugarcoat Rembrandt's vision, because it points to pain that persists even for faithful fathers and mothers. After looking a hundred times at the father in Rembrandt's masterwork, with his hands on the broken son who has lost his left sandal along the way and is clothed only in rags, I see a separateness, an isolation and a tinge of sadness. When I look at the son, I do not see great joy, relief or an embrace signifying a relationship that will nourish the old man in his final days.

I only see everything moving from the father to the son; I see nothing returning from the son. His head and averted face resting near the father's heart tell us nothing except that he is finally able to receive what his beloved father has to offer. There is no indication that he is capable of giving anything back.

Returning to the parable in the Bible,[48] I looked at the descriptive words again: Compassion, running, embracing, kissing, putting on the robe, ring and sandals, killing the fattened calf, eating, celebrating, receiving the son back safe and sound and describing him as dead and now alive–lost and now found. Receiving, restoration, accepting without questioning and love without demanding anything in return all stand out, and they are directed exclusively to the son. We are not told whether the son becomes a true son in heart or even wants to be much more than a servant who is favored above his fellows.

What is the father receiving? Of course he is gladdened, relieved and comforted by his son's return. But Rembrandt seems to portray him with a separation approaching aloof-

---

47   Ibid., 138.
48   Luke 15:11-32.

ness. Why? The parable is *all* about what the father is giving and *little* about what he is receiving. While perfectly free to celebrate, receive and embrace his son while holding nothing whatsoever against him, the father remains strangely isolated. Is this the terrible loneliness and striking fullness that Nouwen describes?

My challenge is to receive the prodigal son, whoever he might be and whenever he might come. And I am to do this without demanding anything in return? Surely biblical scholars can explore other interpretations and applications of this passage. However, if I can live the message that I have received from Henri Nouwen and Rembrandt about becoming a true father, it will be enough.

Will you join me? Will you embark on the journey, even though it involves a dying to dearly held egocentricity? Will you endure the terrible loneliness? Will you embrace the strength, the deep humility, and the powerful touch that become yours when you travel this road? May God the Father help us, for the true mother or father within us will not emerge without his hand upon us.

DYING TO LIVE APPLICATION

Receive the returning person without needing or demanding anything except the privilege of giving love and compassion.

QUESTIONS FOR REFLECTION

Using the idea of *father* as developed in this chapter, do you wish to become a father or mother? Why? Is it worth the cost?

What would it be like to be or become a person like this?

Would you like to have a person like this in your life? Why? What function would he or she fulfill for you? Do you already have someone who fills that role?

CHAPTER 7

✕ ✕ ✕

Esther: That Others May Live

DYING TO LIVE PRINCIPLE
Look at life through a wide-angle lens.

Television and movie star James Garner was working in a car wash before his well known acting career began in 1956 with a bit part on Broadway. Kurt Warner was bagging groceries just before he was signed to play for an Arena League football team in 1995. In 1999, Warner won the Super Bowl as the game MVP. A red-haired girl singing the National Anthem at a rodeo in Oklahoma City was spotted by Red Steagall, a country artist. Steagall brought her to Nashville, and Reba McIntyre's incredible career that produced 50 million-plus albums sold worldwide, Broadway productions, films, and an award-winning television program was launched.

Reading such stories, we may fantasize a little for ourselves, enjoy the sweet taste of success though another, and move on quickly with our lives. But we would do well to ask, "Why?" Why is such unexpected fame given to a few and withheld from so many?

Reba McIntyre's spectacular and unexpected rise is a mere warm up for Esther's story in the Old Testament. Esther and her Uncle Mordecai were part of the Jewish exile community in Persia when Ahasuerus (known as Xerxes) was sovereign. Mordecai, who was exiled in Jeconiah's reign, adopted Esther after her parents died. We know little or nothing about Esther or Mordecai outside the book bearing Esther's name.

After Ahasuerus had been king for three years, he threw a party that lasted for six months. During this time, Ahasuerus deposed his wife, Queen Vashti, because she wouldn't expose herself to a group of drunken royal partygoers. Ahasuerus' court officials decided to conduct a search for the most beautiful and desirable woman in the kingdom, who would then become the new queen.

Esther was less likely to be chosen than was James Garner to be plucked from a car wash, Kurt Warner to be delivered from bagging groceries, or Reba McIntyre to be discovered at an obscure rodeo. No doubt hordes of beautiful women lived throughout the kingdom, which stretched from India to Ethiopia. Many would have had more refined social graces than a protected Jewish girl from a strict religious home. Esther would have been more like the retiring servant girl, Cinderella, than her posturing sisters.

Two truths from my life's inventory apply here. The first is *favor:* a phenomenon occurring broadly in human experience and quite explicitly in God's plan when a person is exalted for no apparent (or at least an insufficient) reason. If God gives favor to you, don't worry about whether you deserve it. Instead, accept it and steward it!

My second truth is quite apparent, if you think about it: *God works in murky waters!* In this amazing, unexpected case, how could God be involved when this Jewish girl volunteered for a brief stint with a pagan king? She had less chance of winning the queen lottery than the least experienced player has in a back alley crap shoot. Somehow, though, God can be present in such embarrassing and contradictory circumstances. Who can explain it? More to the point, who can explain *God?*

The strange narrative continues with the emergence of Haman. It would be charitable to call him an evil, self-centered man. If this were an old Broadway play, Haman would enter with loud booing and hissing by the crowd. With very little provocation on the part of the Jews, the bloodthirsty Haman was able to gain an edict to have Jews exterminated throughout the kingdom.

None of us would choose the situation in which Esther found herself. With Mordecai's counsel "for such a time as this," she concluded, "If I perish, I perish" (Est. 4:14, 16). These two principles—recognizing that extraordinary times call for extraordinary measures and being willing to do the right thing no matter the personal cost—still challenge us to look beyond our own interests when we face a dire situation.

The first is "for such a time as this." Esther's rise to queen of a great empire had little to do with her personal enjoyment. She had attendants to meet her every wish, the best seat for any event, private cooks, a supervisory role, official events with the king and opportunities to develop intellectually, culturally and socially.

There are times, however, when we face only two choices, with no in-betweens, no alternatives. When Esther learned of Haman's plot, this *time, such a time as this, this strategic moment* left her with only two options: speaking up at great personal risk, or remaining silent and allowing a genocide to proceed. Esther was stripped of all other possibilities. She had no means of exiting this deadly situation. Her rise to fame and prominence was for *such a time as this*. All personal considerations were overruled.

If I perish, I perish was the only right conclusion for Esther. The welfare and survival of her people demanded that she place her life on the line. It was her life for theirs or their survival for hers. Her queenship was a mere bargaining chip to avert disaster for the people of God.

The two truths lead us to a single lesson that is as plain as a neon sign in a California café–*my life for others*! Suppose your life is filled with the pleasures that come with limitless funds or resources, the ability to do what you want, and status enjoyed by the extremely select. You are living Esther's situation! At the peak of her success and standing and situation, an awful and unavoidable choice stared her in the face.

Esther's circumstances and ours are strategically granted. *Such a time as this* demands that we think of God and others first. If we instead choose self, disaster or great loss in one form or another is certain.

If I perish, I perish follows close behind. The words themselves are ominous. Could you hear yourself instead praying the following? "Lord, I have so much to live for. Privileges have been entrusted to me that could benefit others in many ways if I could live on for years to come. Lord, the timing is so bad. Finally things have come together so that my life makes sense and seems really worthwhile for me and those around me. So many people are depending on me right now." Of course you could; it is a temptation we all face.

Yet we frequently see those who set aside their lives for others. A soldier will jump on a hand grenade to save his comrades. A mother will drown trying to save her child. A random passerby will die trying to rescue someone from a fire. A citizen donates a vital organ. Someone else steps in front of a bullet intended for another. With some embarrassment, we may wonder, "Why would someone do that for a person she doesn't know?"

A powerful example of the *that others might live* principle occurred in the 15th century. A peasant girl was born on the Feast of Epiphany in 1412 to solid farm parents in Domremy, France. Jeanne la Pucelle died before her 20th birthday on May 29, 1431. And yet all of us know something of her story. When she was an adolescent and dancing in her father's garden with girlfriends, she had a divine encounter. Faithfulness to God was the general content of this first unexpected contact with the Unknown. However, by May 1428, the voice told her that she was to rescue France from invaders and make sure the dauphin was crowned king of France.

Charles VII was the heir of the insane King Charles VI, and Jeanne la Pucelle's task was to guarantee that he inherited the throne of France instead of the English. The English, in league with the Burgundians, were overrunning France.

Yet there was a power vacuum *for such a time as this*. Charles VII was, in the words of one historian, "unusually ugly, physically weak, and a complete coward. He considered the situation hopeless and spent most of his time in frivolous pastimes with his court."[49] Supposedly he would not walk across a bridge for fear it would fall under his weight.

It was for this man and in his place that this girl, whom we know as Joan of Arc, led the French military. It was this man who betrayed her after she led the French to victory. He helped make sure she went to her death after leading the French to triumph in a battle they should never have won. Before she was killed as a 19-year-old, the way was cleared for Charles VII to become king and the English to be routed from France.

No person of good will could wish for this end to Joan. Depending on how violent your thoughts might be, you could

---

49   Walter Walker, *Extraordinary Encounters with God: How Famous People in History Experienced God in Unexpected Ways* (Ann Arbor MI: Servant Publications, 1997), 51.

envision the assassination of Charles VII and a massive outcry from every corner of France that Joan of Arc should become ruler and sit on the throne of France as her queen.

You would never under any circumstances have Charles VII on the throne. It would be kind and generous to call him a failed leader. Evil upon evil and shame upon shame, he conspired with the Church, the Burgundians and the English for her to fail and eventually go to the stake. With deep sadness, most anyone would ask, "Lord, how could you ask this young woman to deliver an entire nation and ensure the crowning of a despicable king who betrayed her? Is she to sacrifice her life with no reward whatsoever and to be burned like a piece of garbage?"

Sadly, the story of Joan of Arc is not one of a kind. Troubled, tortured or anguished cries have risen from the broken hearts of God's people through the centuries. "Lord, I don't understand this. How could you permit such a thing? It seems irrational, cruel, unnecessary and completely unwarranted." We have developed a field of theology called theodicy in which we attempt to justify the ways of God with men. Why does God allow evil and suffering? More personally, we wonder whether a loving God will allow such a miserable end to happen to us.

As a restless, adventuring type person, one of my personal dreads is ending up in diapers at a local nursing home. It is much more appealing to think about taking a bullet in the head in some fierce, kingdom-related conflict. I sometimes think of advancing the gospel in the Muslim world and dying in the process. It wouldn't even be necessary to recover my body. I know I am loved by my family, whether they have my remains or not. I would rather withstand a few moments of agony than become that old man in the nursing home.

However, some years ago I made a commitment that can be expressed in this statement: "Lord, if it is for your greatest glory for me to become that helpless, disheveled old man, count me in. However, I hope you have other plans!" But we can trust God's plans even when they don't match ours.

While spending time in Florida a few weeks after writing this, something happened which was totally outside my plans for this welcome mid-winter reprieve. I became gravely ill with a very dangerous blood sepsis or infection. For a short while, I ended up wearing the "diaper" and a "bag" for bodily fluids.

To be sure, this desperate medical situation became a form of dying which I felt deeply. But it was much more – an invaluable equipping for this stage of my life in which my grip was loosened on expectations for a very long, active and pleasurable life to which I had clung tenaciously. This is a welcome freedom!

A portion of a great hymn, "God Moves in a Mysterious Way," has floated in my memory for many years. "Ye fearful saints, fresh courage take. The clouds you so much dread are big with mercy and shall break in blessings on your head." While we understand this retrospectively with great saints such as Joan of Arc, we can also grasp it for our own lives and those we love.

Some years ago I looked up into the face of a young and gifted surgeon. That was the last thing I remember before being wheeled into surgery–his kind and handsome face stays in my memory. Now my surgeon and a certain megachurch pastor were best of friends. They were both athletes. They jointly owned a boat and went water skiing together frequently.

Then the unthinkable happened. This exceptional young doctor and the highly respected woman married to the pastor both developed horrible cancers that led to terrible deaths while their heartbroken spouses looked on helplessly. Sometime later, however, the surviving husband and wife (who was also a doctor) fearfully asked the question, "Should we consider becoming a new husband-wife team without ever forgetting for a moment the ones we loved so dearly?" They answered, "Yes!," and I met them years later at our granddaughter's wedding.

The stories pile up for me. Recently, I spoke with an outstanding Christian who leads a strategic charity. She mentioned seeing a former president of an internationally known Christian college. I remember him as tall and athletic. She said sadly, "He has Alzheimer's. He still has his smile, but what he says doesn't make sense."

I followed this unwanted story with a query about one of the people in my pantheon of heroes, an author who is one of the more powerful speakers I have heard. The ministry leader's answer was like a cloud drifting over the sun: "Her mind is completely gone. She too has Alzheimer's!"

So I don't understand why God did what he did with Joan of Arc, and my grasp is just as lacking for the people in these stories. But my heart burns with passion to finish well. I plead with God to keep this most unworthy and often unfaithful child of his faithful to the end—by his strength, which can make mine sufficient. And, if this is true, I believe I can say, "Lord, I have no need to negotiate over the manner of my dying. You know me and what plan you have determined in a love that goes far beyond when I was born and when I will die. Do what will best lift up the name of him who died for me!"

Here is a footnote to Joan of Arc's story. Charles VII, the despicable king who betrayed the very woman who fought in his place to deliver France from foreigners, could have lived out his years with borrowed favor from Joan, finding even greater freedom to live a frivolous and cowardly life. But a historian reports, "Afterward, due in large part to Joan's influence, it was Charles VII who 'recanted' his ways. He changed his indulgent lifestyle and actually became a serious, hard-working monarch. He even chose some of Joan's knights as his advisors. Eventually, the English were completely routed from France, fulfilling Joan's vision."[50]

If the Lord chooses our particular dying, who knows what the eventual result might be? It may be a hard case like that of Charles VII, who is finally awakened from his stupor. Or it might be an LPN charged with changing the dreaded diaper for an aged person, who finds the pathway to life eternal through a shattered individual who still radiates a little of the glory of God.

You have considered the life and dying of Joan of Arc and probably referenced your own as well. How might you pray? What is the desire that is deeper than what you dread?

Then there is Amy Carmichael. I happened to ask a client if he had ever heard of her. His response took me completely off guard. Both of us have daughters named after this extraordinary woman. Elizabeth Elliot's graceful biography about Amy Carmichael has the best possible title, *A Chance to Die*.[51] And die is exactly what Carmichael did throughout her long career in India. Despite the fact that not many Indians I speak with know of her today, this Irish woman's hand still rests on the rudder

---

50   Walker, *Extraordinary Encounters with God*, 58.

51   Elisabeth Elliot, *A Chance to Die: The Life and Legacy of Amy Carmichael* (Old Tappan, NJ: Revell 1987; Grand Rapids: Revell, 2005). The material that follows in the text is drawn from this biography.

of Indian life. Laws enacted in her district to protect weak and helpless children are now taken for granted throughout India.

Carmichael was born into a beautiful Christian home in the west of Ireland (Donegal) in 1867. She grew up like a flower that blossomed for God from girlhood to the grave. In Belfast she reached out to the *shawlies* (factory girls and homeless people who received their names because of the shawls they wore) and ragamuffin children. Soon 300 of these people were attracted to her ministry, and the Welcome Evangelical Church was formed. Carmichael was an aggressive and bold Christian leader who cultivated a hidden and deep life with God.

In her childhood journals, Carmichael selected as her *nome de plume-nobody!* During the course of her life, she fastidiously guarded her desire and practice to be a nobody for the King of Kings. She avoided recognition as if it were a disease. Carmichael descended to the depths of *nobodiness* for others.

When Carmichael heard Hudson Taylor, the great modern day apostle to inland China, speak in 1887, she soon sensed her own call. Although she was a poor candidate as a missionary anywhere, let alone Asia, Carmichael wanted to serve with him. She suffered from neuralgia, a disease of the nerves. Perhaps we would call it fibromyalgia today-a disease that produces weakness and achiness and sometimes landed Amy in bed for weeks.

After a stint in Japan that ended when her health failed, this unlikely candidate eventually arrived in Tamil Nadu in India, just 30 miles from its southern tip. To relate better to the nationals, she followed the Hudson Taylor model and dressed in saris as they did. She dyed her skin with coffee to more closely identify with her adopted people. She had prayed for blue eyes like other Irish girls when she was very young. Now she understood why her prayer was denied!

The focus of Carmichael's ministry was fixed when she learned of the horrors of forced temple prostitution and servitude for girls (sometimes boys as well). She formed the Dohnavur Fellowship and in her lifetime saw more than a thousand children delivered from hopeless situations.

Carmichael wrote 35 published books. They exhibit a deep, mystical relationship with God and great creativity. They powerfully draw readers into deeper relationship with and service to the Lord. Her ministry, with a complex of buildings and facilities, continues even today.

What was the cost to Amy Carmichael? She died in 1951 after 56 years without a furlough. She was never truly healthy. A fall in 1931 limited her further, and she was bedridden for much of her remaining life. Marriage was never an option.

I sometimes wonder how much of the massive missionary work done today by both expatriates and nationals in some way relates to Carmichael's pioneering work. She lived her motto, "One can give without loving, but one cannot love without giving." A young woman wrote and asked Carmichael what missionary life was like. She wrote back, *Missionary life is simply a chance to die.*"

Carmichael lived this out even in her dying at age 83. She asked that no stone be put over her grave. When she was buried in this manner, the girls who had been rescued from tragic lives put a bird bath over her place of interment with the single word inscription, *Amma*. In the Tamil language, it means *mother*. She certainly was a mother in her living, loving others, passionately pursuing life with Christ, and in her dying.

If *a chance to die* sums up Carmichael's career, it is equally correct to assume *that others may live* is a net result of her life. Carmichael's life provided innumerable opportunities for others to live; and it continues to do so as a result of her lasting influence. In a sense, she was an Esther, placed by God *for such a time as this*. Now let me ask *you* a question: To what extent is your life being lived so *that others may live*?

DYING TO LIVE APPLICATION

Confront what you dread to become more powerfully available to God for others.

QUESTIONS FOR REFLECTION

Have you considered your life as a potential opportunity for others to live?

What motivation do you find to live in this manner?

What might this look like for you? What kind of results could you envision?

PART TWO

Marketplace Lessons

CHAPTER 8

Peter: The Empty Net Night on the Sea of Galilee

DYING TO LIVE PRINCIPLE

Persevere through the dark places to a sunrise encounter with the risen Christ.

We noted early in our conversation that the contents of this book represent what I would like to say to the company owners and presidents I serve but can't in the short time we have together. A few weeks after the manuscript was finished, I sat with seasoned business leaders in a beautiful retreat center and we began by sharing our stories. Jackson (name changed) volunteered and I believe his story could be summarized in the film title, *Perfect Storm*.

A fishing boat off the northeast coast of the U.S. is caught in a meteorological phenomena in which two weather fronts and a hurricane converge in the path of the trawler, Andrea Gail. The crew takes the risk of racing back to shore directly through this monumental storm to preserve their full catch after the ship ice machine breaks down threatening the loss of all the fish they had in the hold.

Jackson's company was caught in a perfect business storm in which during a period of a few months, a profitable and favorable economic environment became a nightmare. He bought out siblings at the market high in 2007. The company was a two generation fixture in the Chicago area.

Jackson's assets were depleted and a large bank line was needed to cover the purchase and the ongoing demands of a capital intense business. The *perfect storm* began to blow with its fury in 2008. Already strapped for cash, Jackson's market area began to dry up. The pie was cut in half for all the suppliers in the Chicago market.

A final element of this perfect storm story came when the company lost its distributorship arrangement with the manufacturer they represented. The company was now lost and its descent to the graveyard was only a matter of time and a question of how many millions of dollars would be lost.

The final blow came when Jackson was notified that he had eight hours to decide whether or not he would put his home up for collateral. The counsel he gained in this brief window was defective and he agreed. From being president of an established company with nearly a hundred employees to presiding over an operation with millions of dollars in debt and the potential of his home being taken out from under him was his situation in just a few short months.

He was highly respected in the Christian community. His work included being president of a large Christian organization for a while, which served hundreds of families in Illinois. None of the positives in his charmed life changed any of the outcomes that were crashing down on him.

His story introduced the theme of our retreat–*The empty net syndrome.* John 21 records the Peter-led fishing expedition after our Lord was raised from the dead and appeared twice before to the disciples.

Like Jackson, they came up empty handed. The Gospel of John is painting the picture of a group of men who had no place to return to and no place to go. Accepting the call of Christ made them has-beens for every other endeavor and damaged property for any future career considerations. The Savior's call led to too many burnt bridges.

Here is the Apostle John's account from John 21:1-14:

After these things Jesus manifested Himself again to the disciples at the Sea of Tiberias, and He manifested Himself in this way. Simon Peter, and Thomas called Didymus, and Nathanael of Cana in Galilee, and the sons of Zebedee, and two others of His disciples were together. Simon Peter said to them, "I am going fishing." They said to him, "We will also come with you." They went out and got into the boat; and that night they caught nothing. But when the day was now breaking, Jesus stood on the beach; yet the disciples did not know that it was Jesus. So Jesus said to them, "Children, you do not have any fish, do you?" They answered Him, "No." And He said to them, "Cast the net on the right-hand side of the boat and you will find a catch." So they cast, and then they were not able to haul it in because of the great number of fish. Therefore that disciple whom Jesus loved said to Peter, "It is the Lord." So when Simon Peter heard that it was the Lord, he put his outer garment on (for he was stripped for work), and threw himself into the sea. But the other disciples came in the little boat, for they were not far from the land, but about one hundred yards away, dragging the net full of fish. So when they got out on the land, they saw a charcoal fire already laid and fish placed on it, and bread. Jesus said to them, "Bring some of the fish which you have now caught." Simon Peter went up and drew the net to land, full of large fish, a hundred and fifty-three; and although there were so many, the net was not torn. Jesus said to them, "Come and have breakfast." None of the disciples ventured to question Him, "Who are You?" knowing that it was the Lord. Jesus came and took the bread and gave it to them, and the fish likewise. This is now the third time that Jesus was manifested to the disciples, after He was raised from the dead.

This is Peter's empty net adventure. He led the way in returning to his old occupation and in running to the resurrected Lord when he catapulted himself overboard to be the first to get there.

Empty net experiences permeate the biographies (written and unwritten) of Christian experience. I caught the bold print in a current *Christianity Today*[52] which noted that both Jonathan Edwards (perhaps our greatest American theologian) and John Calvin were banished from their churches. Jonathan Edwards (president of Harvard for a while) spent an empty net period in a frontier area of New England where his family was in danger of being massacred by Indians after he was expelled from his fashionable and influential pastorate. His poverty was so severe that he had no money for paper and did some of his writing in the margins of books.

What does an empty net experience look like? What happens when everything goes south as it did with Jackson or innumerable other Christians? What does it or can it involve? We attempted to describe what people experience and came up with some of the following ideas: Fear, dread, loss of hope or hopelessness, futility ("I put it all on the line, gave it my best and it all comes to nothing."), rage, anger, bitterness, jealousy,

---

52   Jennifer Powell McNutt, "The Enduring Church," *Christianity Today*, January 2011, 47.

envy, resentment or even hatred ("Why does someone else who worked *less*, is not as smart or not as faithful have a wonderfully full net and I am getting nothing but kicked around?"), emptiness–life emptied out and no RX to change it, the 3 D's of discouragement, disappointment or depression, bankrupt, pervasive feeling of being a loser, darkness–night of the soul, raw hurt, meaninglessness–"I thought I found answers but came up empty or out of control without the ability to get things back on track."

While ours may last much longer, Peter's and the other disciple's empty net shift lasted only a night and it was immediately followed by a sunrise with a catered breakfast prepared by the Lord himself. We discussed whether or not this was a penultimate experience–a permanent high point in all of their lives. Peter had been to the Mount of Transfiguration, seen five thousand and then four thousand more fed, the dead raised and innumerable other happenings as he followed the Lord for the past three and a half years. It is Peter who is immortalized by his confession that Jesus is the Christ, the Son of the living God in Matthew 16:16. Yet, this had to be special, very special even among every other occurrence in which he played a role.

Yet, follow Peter's life to the end and what will you discover? You will find that the sunrise after an empty net night had a net result. It was part of Peter's dying to live process for what was to come–what will comprise the greatest, most significant and strategic contribution of his life. A cold, uncomfortable and fruitless night on the water (with which every commercial fisherman is familiar) had to precede the remainder of his life in which he rose to take his place among the greatest spiritual leaders in either Old or New Testaments.

Pentecost was days away (Acts 2). Peter was the prime player and leader during this spectacular formative period in these early days of the infant church. He wasn't finished yet. He wrote the two towering epistles that bear his name. They testify to the reality that he has become the transformed apostle. They have influenced uncounted thousands in the two millennia since he wrote them.

He had one final leg of his journey ahead of him. The year of his death and circumstances cannot be determined with certainty. His death is frequently dated at AD 64 or 65 in Rome during the Neronian persecution. Commonly accepted tradition has it that he was sentenced to crucifixion and that he requested to be nailed upside down to a cross out of deference to his Lord and Savior who was crucified upright.

Peter's empty net night was not followed by an endless stream of pleasant sunrises. It was just another preparation to go all the way through to an end that called for monumental perseverance.

Jackson–the outstanding business leader and company president, husband, father and public Christian leader–had it all and lost it quickly. His empty net experience was severe. His net was full and in a few months empty.

Yet, he affirmed twice in our retreat what we have been saying for a book. In a matter of fact way that belied his stress and suffering over the past couple of years, he said essentially, "There is no way that I could have grown as I have without this devastating experience." Perhaps he will be prepared for a much less prominent career but a much more significant life than he could have experienced without his net being emptied.

What about John Calvin and Jonathan Edwards and a host of others throughout church history? Could they have ever become who they turned out to be without empty net experiences and a life of dying to live as they were pushed into greatness and immortality in the Kingdom?

So then, do you have a steady secure life, a stream of superb sunrises to light up your life, a place in the sun as leader, influencer for Christ and the Kingdom and other privileges grafted generously into your life? Have you arrived by all reasonable standards?

You may yet have a mighty distance to go in order to get all the way and climb to the top of the mountain you are assigned. You may have to go the way of the planted seed and the night of the empty net to get to the next sunrise before you go on, go higher and go all the way.

Stumbling Simon became transformed and triumphant Peter for all the generations who follow him. In his first epistle which focuses on suffering in the context of our immense privileges, he assures us of available grace to make it possible to win as he did. He does not focus on himself but uses his experiences as recorded in the New Testament to serve us today:

> Blessed be the God and Father of our Lord Jesus Christ, who according to His great mercy has caused us to be born again to a living hope through the resurrection of Jesus Christ from the dead, to obtain an inheritance which is imperishable and undefiled and will not fade away, reserved in heaven for you, who are protected by the power of God through faith for a salvation ready to be revealed in the last time. In this you greatly rejoice, even though now for a little while, if necessary, you have been distressed by various trials, so that the proof of your faith, being more precious than gold which is perishable, even though tested by fire, may be found to

result in praise and glory and honor at the revelation of Jesus Christ. (I Peter 1:3-7)

After you have suffered for a little while, the God of all grace, who called you to His eternal glory in Christ, will Himself perfect, confirm, strengthen and establish you. (I Peter 5:10)

The life he points us to is bigger than the empty nets along the way and we are surely intended to outlast the night as he did on the Sea of Galilee after which he went all the way to an upside down death (if tradition is accurate) on a cross in Rome.

DYING TO LIVE APPLICATION

No matter how many empty net nights may be ahead, under-stand that your sunrise will exceed them all.

QUESTIONS FOR REFLECTION

When you read this chapter, were you reminded of a painfully emptying chapter in your life?

How would you characterize an empty net experience?

Why is a dark and empty period both dangerous and also a potentially strategic and life-changing part of your journey?

.

CHAPTER 9

❤ ❤ ❤

Paul (Acts): Life as an Expendable Commodity

DYING TO LIVE PRINCIPLE
*Life is raised to a higher power when
lived as an expendable commodity.*

One of our sons has a somewhat cynical take on seniors who move to Florida or spend winters there, as we do for a few weeks each winter. He wryly says that they are seeking a warm place to die. While my son is overstating for effect, there is a lot of truth in his observation of a not uncommon lifestyle–extending one's life in the most pleasant way possible as an *end in itself.* But for those of us who are dying to live, mere life extension is not a valid option. We need a reason to live or a cause big enough to make life an expendable commodity.

The classic statement of this principle is found in Acts 20:24.

I do not consider my life of any account as dear to myself, so that I may finish my course and the ministry which I received from the Lord Jesus, to testify solemnly of the gospel of the grace of God.

This declaration comes late in Paul's career. He is heading back to Jerusalem, toward a future that he cannot foresee. He is *finished*–finished with his third missionary trip, finished in Greece, finished in Philippi and Thessalonica in Macedonia, and finished with whatever he was doing in Asia Minor when he almost died before coming over to northern Macedonia.

"Job well done, Paul!" we might be expected to cheer at this point. "Time for some R & R." I would have gladly contributed funds to the beloved apostle for an extended time to rest and recharge. I sometimes think about returning to favorite spots in Greece and the islands and just hanging out for a while. Maybe it was temporarily time for Paul to get off the career treadmill and soak up some sun. He seemed to be heading straight for a premature death. But no—the Apostle Paul was far more driven than I am. Being a "lay about" even for a short time was not for him.

On this journey to Jerusalem, he is moving rapidly. He has decided to bypass Ephesus in Asia, where he experienced so much trouble, sparking a near riot.[53] He stops at Miletus, down the coast of modern Turkey from Ephesus and not very far from Patmos, where the great Apostle John will be exiled in a few years. From there, he calls the Ephesian elders to him. At this emotional gathering, he reminds them of the momentous time he spent with them—which involved danger and deliverance. Paul spent two years in Ephesus and conducted his now famous training program at the school of Tyrannus.

Walk the streets of ancient Ephesus today and you will marvel at one of the most spectacular excavations from the ancient world. You will reflect reverently on the apostolic presence there, which resulted in one of the great epistles in the New Testament—Ephesians. Paul's poignant word to the elders of the Ephesian church at Miletus, as recorded by Luke the physician in Acts 20:17-38, provide the context for his razor-sharp pronouncement.

> You yourselves know, from the first day that I set foot in Asia, how I was with you the whole time, serving the Lord with all humility and with tears and with trials which came upon me through the plots

---

53   See Acts 19:23-41.

of the Jews; how I did not shrink from declaring to you anything that was profitable, and teaching you publicly and from house to house, solemnly testifying to both Jews and Greeks of repentance toward God and faith in our Lord Jesus Christ. And now, behold, bound by the Spirit, I am on my way to Jerusalem, not knowing what will happen to me there, except that the Holy Spirit solemnly testifies to me in every city, saying that bonds and afflictions await me. *But I do not consider my life of any account as dear to myself, so that I may finish my course and the ministry which I received from the Lord Jesus, to testify solemnly of the Gospel of the grace of God.*[54]

Do you feel grief for the apostle when you read this?

"Paul, bypass Jerusalem for now," we might counsel him with the best of intentions. "Travel a few miles north to the resort area of Ramallah. Think, pray, regain your strength before you step into the treacherous murkiness of Jerusalem." This would be good advice, except for this one inescapable fact. Paul would have had none of it. He was dying to live.

The Ephesian church leaders felt much the same way we do, only with greater intensity.

When he had said these things, he knelt down and prayed with them all. And they began to weep aloud and embraced Paul, and repeatedly kissed him, grieving especially over the word which he had spoken, that they would not see his face again. And they were accompanying him to the ship.[55]

---

54   Acts 20:18-24, italics mine.
55   Acts 20:36-38.

All of us eventually must say goodbye—even those who seek to save their lives, who are living simply to live. Yet this reality should not make us stoic and void of emotion. It certainly did not for Paul, nor for the Christians he encountered on the way to Jerusalem. Their concern was expressed all the way to Caesarea.

> When we had finished the voyage from Tyre, we arrived in Ptolemais... On the next day we left and came to Caesarea ... As we were staying there for some days, a prophet named Agabus came down from Judea. And coming to us, he took Paul's belt and bound his own feet and hands, and said, "This is what the Holy Spirit says: 'In this way the Jews at Jerusalem will bind the man who owns this belt and deliver him into the hands of the Gentiles.'" When we had heard this, we as well as the local residents began begging him not to go up Jerusalem. Then Paul answered, "What are you doing, weeping and breaking my heart? For I am ready not only to be bound, but even to die at Jerusalem for the name of the Lord Jesus." And since he would not be persuaded, we fell silent, remarking, "The will of the Lord be done!"[56]

While this wrenching, heartbreaking series of goodbyes continues, Paul's resolve does not falter. Is the road dreary, desolate and deserted for those of us who are willing to die to live? Must we simply endure what must come to pass, teetering on the edge of hopelessness and depression? Paul knew what was coming when he wrote Timothy during his second imprison-

---

56   Acts 21:7-8, 10-14.

ment in Rome: "I am already being poured out as a drink offering, and the time of my departure has come."[57]

Yet under house arrest in Rome, Paul writes the Book of Philippians, the most joyful and upbeat of all his letters! In it the idea of joy occurs at least 18 times. One commentator's outline uses this theme for the whole book: "*Rejoicing* in Christ's service" for chapter 1; "*rejoicing* in Christ's selflessness" for chapter 2; "*rejoicing* in Christ's sufferings" for chapter 3; and "*rejoicing* in Christ's sufficiency" for chapter 4.[58]

How can this paradoxical existence of death and joy be possible? Focusing on living for God's purpose in dark moments, giving yourself for an awesome, worthwhile or fulfilling purpose, and experiencing life as an expendable commodity bring joy. That's because it both kills our old ambitions while resurrecting us to new ones. Look again at what the apostle said in the theme verse for this chapter, this time using the New International Version.

> However, I consider my life worth nothing to me, if only I may finish the race and complete the task the Lord Jesus has given me–the task of testifying to the gospel of God's grace.[59]

The translation "worth nothing to me" seemed like an exaggeration until I looked at the Greek and found the idea reinforced. Comparing the NASB rendering side by side with the NIV helps us evaluate Paul's passionate statement more carefully. Here is the NASB:

---

57   2 Timothy 4:6.
58   Harold L. Willmington, *Willmington's Guide to the Bible* (Wheaton: Tyndale House, 1997), 710.
59   Acts 20:24, NIV (1984).

I do not consider my life of any account as dear to myself, so that I may finish my course and the ministry which I received from the Lord Jesus, to testify solemnly of the gospel of the grace of God.

It makes no difference what version you use. Paul's purpose for his life is unmistakable. We see a couple of points:

1. Paul is not riding on emotion. The wording rendered *to consider* in the original includes the idea of mathematical precision. It is a word an accountant would use. Paul's conclusion about his life is passionate, yes, but it is far more. It is a determination made deep within his being. It stands whether he is being feted as a hero or cast into prison. Willmington notes, "Paul was imprisoned in Rome's Mamertine Prison, which had only two cells, one below the other, with Paul occupying the lower cell."[60] Many believe that Paul wrote 2 Timothy from there during his second imprisonment in Rome.

   The obvious question for you and me is how deeply we have integrated the same perspective into our lives. We need to say (and mean), *"My life is expendable!"* It can be administered, apportioned, doled out, given away, disbursed, dispensed, or distributed where it is supposed to go for the master purpose that overrides all others.

2. Paul tells us essentially, "Be as definitive as you can." Don't simply hide behind his great affirmation without finding something that grips your soul as his terminal conclusion did for him. Your purpose may be

---

60   Ibid. 739.

focused a little differently as you move through stages of your life. It will be influenced by your gifts or calling. Paul's purpose statement in Acts relates to his calling as an apostle and teacher. Yours will not be exactly the same.

Paul then summons the Ephesian elders to their own calling—a pastoral one. In so doing, he uses his own experience as leverage and includes a powerful promise to further encourage them. He is calling these spiritual leaders to view their lives as expendable commodities to fulfill the role God has assigned to them.

And now, behold, I know that none of you among whom I have gone about proclaiming the kingdom will see my face again. Therefore I testify to you this day that I am innocent of the blood of all of you, for I did not shrink from declaring to you the whole counsel of God. Pay careful attention to yourselves and to all the flock, in which the Holy Spirit has made you overseers, to care for the church of God, which he obtained with his own blood. I know that after my departure fierce wolves will come in among you, not sparing the flock; and from among your own selves will arise men speaking twisted things, to draw away the disciples after them. Therefore be alert, remembering that for three years I did not cease night or day to admonish everyone with tears. And now I commend you to God and to the word of his grace, which is able to build you up and to give you the inheritance among all those who are sanctified.[61]

---

61   Acts 20:25-32, ESV.

Each of us (with God's gracious provision) must find that gripping purpose, plan, and passion at the core of our being that can master our lives so that we become expendable. Søren Kierkegaard said, "The thing is to understand myself, to see what God really wishes me to do ... to find the idea for which I can live and die."[62] Richard Hicks claims that "the saddest men I know are the men who have no real vision for their lives. The man who goes to work every day, comes home, reads the paper, has dinner, watches television, and goes to bed— only to repeat the pattern the next day—is not alive or well. Life has been reduced to mere functioning and maintaining."[63]

At one point, I spent a year and a half mulling over the *purpose* for my life, how this was to be expressed in *vision,* and worked out in *mission*. The process of discovery varies for each of us, but the goal is the same: *"What is that vision, plan or purpose that makes my life expendable to reach it?"*

Here is a further note on Paul's great affirmation in Acts 20:24. In one version, "complete the task" is the wording. In the other, "finish my course" is the idea. The original word in the New Testament is critical. It has the idea not of perfection, but of completeness, without a major defect. In this sense, we could say that a car has all four tires, even though one may need balancing. Your house is wired, even though one circuit blows fuses. The issue is whether something is operative, not whether it is perfect. Paul fully completed what God gave him to do; he did so faithfully whether or not it was done flawlessly. The same kind of task is given to us, and we need to remember

---

62   Søren Kierkegaard, Letter to Peter Wilhelm Lund dated August 31, 1835, http://en.wikipedia.org/wiki/Existentialism.

63   Richard Hicks, *The Masculine Journey (Understanding the Six Stages of Manhood)*, NAV Press, Colorado Springs, CO, 1995, 132.

that we can be faithful to complete it, even as we necessarily will fall short of perfection.

I have an athletic windbreaker that says "finisher" on it. I am careful not to wear my prized jacket in some places, because the honor is undeserved. I only have it because my son gave it to me. He finished an Ironman triathlon–something I will never do. The requirements are staggering. Two or three thousand swimmers jump into the water at about 7:00 a.m. Some panic and quit within the first five minutes. The rest swim 2.4 miles, while most of us have never covered even a half-mile in a comfortable pool or calm lake.

Then the contestants are helped out of their wetsuits and run to their bikes to ride 110 miles. They may face hilly terrain or wind or heat that can push some to a near-death experience. Then they must ride into the compound with hundreds of other contestants. Then the final cruel segment begins–running a full marathon–26.2 miles!

A woman with whom my son trained crossed the finish line in a semiconscious state–not too unusual for this race! Many collapse and are taken to a medical tent. Each runner finds a volunteer at each shoulder to help with whatever is needed as he or she crosses the finish line. As the athletes cross, a well-known announcer says with unmistakable compassion and love, "You're an iron man!"

Everyone is hailed just for finishing. Those who finish in the greatest pain or with the slowest times are given equal honor. Many take 12 to 14 hours or longer to complete the race—but they finish! Seventeen hours is the cutoff, and some finish at the last second. Awesome commitment and passion characterize these "iron people."

Like iron man competitors, we are called to identify our ruling passion as the Apostle Paul did and ... *finish*! That is all—just finish.

So find what makes your life expendable and expend it. Finish well–don't die in the backstretch or live a diverted life until you die. May God help you and me to *finish*!

DYING TO LIVE APPLICATION

Identify, commit to and steward the ruling passion with which you are to live with God.

QUESTIONS FOR REFLECTION

Since we instinctively hold onto our lives, why should we consider them as expendable?

Have you seen anyone who was willing to live with his or her life on the line consistently? Do you think they were winners or losers?

Comment on how you have wrestled with what it means to visualize your life as an expendable commodity and your process of integrating this radical principle into your life.

CHAPTER 10

❁ ❁ ❁

Paul (Philippians): From the Red Carpet to the Mountain Top

DYING TO LIVE PRINCIPLE
The Lord partners with you *in* your *ascent.*

An annual ritual captures the attention of millions. It is the *red carpet* phase of the Oscars. The female stars pose in their gorgeous (and sometimes outlandish) attire on the arms of their handsome male escorts. Many of us have sat spellbound for the next three hours while candidates in multiple categories are honored. Culminations come as the envelopes are opened, the winners are announced, and their grateful acceptance speeches are offered.

May I share a secret about *you*? You have wanted your own red carpet recognition, and likely still do. This is quite natural. Unfortunately, we don't always get the red carpet treatment, even when we deserve it. Maybe you cooked a great dish for the church dinner and no one complimented you, not even your husband. Perhaps you pulled off a great feat at work that took a lot out of you, but your boss received all the credit.

On the other hand, perhaps you have had many opportunities to take an intoxicating stroll down the red carpet. Your children realized the terrific cost you and your wife paid to raise them well and position them for success. On a special occasion you were honored; the guests rose to their feet spontaneously when you entered the room, and you could hardly fight back your tears.

Sometimes I find deep emotions rising within when others are lauded for some great accomplishment. I am identifying with these people, experiencing their honor vicariously because of my residual hunger for recognition.

Some of the biblical characters whose stories we have studied enjoyed red carpet opportunities of the highest order. However, it should be obvious by now that those who are dying to live can treat a red carpet experience in only one way–as a way stop or a pause along the way. These events or incidents cannot be our grand finale.

The Apostle Paul hurdled this psychological barrier and never looked back. This sometimes happens with those who have had radical conversions. Paul models the life of someone dying to live. That doesn't mean you should expect to rise to the same heights he did, however. Of the multitudes who attempt Mount Everest in any given year, only a very few reach the top. The apostle's message in Philippians applies: "With the liberal supply of grace that God gives and the help of others, overcome every obstacle you can and climb as far as you are able."

The apostle was no stranger to red carpet experiences. He was successful, recognized by his peers and not embarrassed to admit that he performed at a higher level. He is bold enough to say that if anyone could depend on their ability to produce, he was the man! He was a mover and a shaker before he came to faith in his Messiah.

Do you have a picture album of red carpet incidents that warm your heart? Do you have a place in the sun that brings a deep and steady sense of fulfillment? Be careful; even red carpet experiences may not be all that they're cracked up to be.

For example, in 2010 Sandra Bullock stood on the red carpet as a star among the stars. She was about to receive her first Oscar for *Blind Side,* a long-shot movie. My wife, however, noted that she seemed a little subdued when receiving her Oscar, which represented the pinnacle of her career. That's because Sandra Bullock knew what we didn't: her marriage which had been a source of strength, stability and support was on the verge of imploding. Her husband's affair with a porn star and other women soon surfaced and destroyed their marriage. Bullock's bright moment on the red carpet was clouded to say the least.

The small and select circle of business leaders I serve are prepared to face challenges and difficulties in order to win the bigger battle and grow up. A further and penetrating question is whether or not their place in the sun is sacrosanct as a gift from God that won't be revoked. It is the issue of whether or not the specially prepared, unique and superb blessing they enjoy are somehow reserved and roped off, "the domain or territory of _____!"

There is a passage in Philippians in which the aging Apostle Paul shares what dying to live looks like. I have no illusions about reaching this level of life myself, but I do want my spiritual binoculars to be focused on the heights where he is climbing. Paul stands on his Everest and makes his proclamation:

> If anyone else has a mind to put confidence in the flesh,
> I far more: circumcised the eighth day, of the nation of
> Israel, of the tribe of Benjamin, a Hebrew of Hebrews;
> as to the Law, a Pharisee; as to zeal, a persecutor of the

church; as to the righteousness which is in the Law, found blameless.[64]

Paul then describes his new life in just a few verses. They have burned like an eternal flame since the saints in the Roman colony of Philippi read them nearly two millennia ago.

But whatever things were gain to me, those things I have counted as loss for the sake of Christ. More than that, I count all things to be loss in view of the surpassing value of knowing Christ Jesus my Lord, for whom I have suffered the loss of all things, and count them but rubbish so that I may gain Christ, and may be found in Him, not having a righteousness of my own derived from the Law, but that which is through faith in Christ, the righteousness which comes from God on the basis of faith, that I may know Him and the power of His resurrection and the fellowship of His sufferings, being conformed to His death; in order that I may attain to the resurrection from the dead.[65]

This successful, driven and overachieving man states the personal reversal we are discussing throughout this book. Paul finds a different life center, a radical focus that invalidates what he followed passionately in his previous life. What he saw as gain–what he valued–what he discerned that gave him a place in the sun or placed him on the red carpet—is now disposable. His gain becomes his loss. His new north pole supersedes the old.

Howard Hendricks of Dallas Seminary once observed that we sometimes look at the Bible as though looking through

---

64   Phil. 3:4b-6.
65   Phil. 3:7-11.

the wrong end of a telescope. We see what is real, sweaty and gritty as far away–stylized, anaesthetized and unreal. So let's turn the telescope around and feel the loss of the apostle, what it cost him and the volcanic change that occurred when the Lord Jesus Christ knocked him to the ground on the way to Damascus. Did Paul ever grieve what he was leaving behind?

Loss! Negation and dispossession! Annulment and abolishment! These terms describe what happened to Paul from the internal to the external layers of his life. Radical changes became permanent in his attitudes, motivations, incentives, direction, aspirations and goals. Looking up from our place several base camps below, we might say, "Oh, Beloved Apostle, put your hands on my head and pray that I might continue to climb until, like you, I reach a glorious end of *my* pilgrimage." Listen again to his words!

> But whatever things were gain to me, those things I have counted as loss for the sake of Christ. More than that, I count all things to be loss in view of the surpassing value of knowing Christ Jesus my Lord, for whom I have suffered the loss of all things, and count them but rubbish so that I may gain Christ, and may be found in Him.

This is the polarizing power of Christ that brings a new north, south, east and west. The pinnacle of the apostle's life became the pit. What was gain became loss. His red carpets became mud mats. Unless a radical experience similar to the apostle's is pushed on us, our journey is likely to be more of a consistent climb, with crises, pivot points or critical choices thrown in from time to time. Paul is asking us for an *attitude* and a *responsiveness to God,* not necessarily a radical crisis.

Paul doesn't beat us up because we are still at a base camp below him. In fact, he admits he *himself* has not *arrived*. In Paul's reckoning, he hasn't reached the pinnacle of life with Christ, but he presses on:

> Brethren, I do not regard myself as having laid hold of it yet; but one thing I do: forgetting what lies behind and reaching forward to what lies ahead, I press on toward the goal for the prize of the upward call of God in Christ Jesus. Let us therefore, as many as are perfect, have this attitude; and if in anything you have a different attitude, God will reveal that also to you; however, let us keep living by that same standard to which we have attained.
>
> Brethren, join in following my example, and observe those who walk according to the pattern you have in us.[66]

Observe Paul's gracious, loving and encouraging attitude. He is helping us along, not whipping us from behind. He is saying, "God has your back. If you are slipping up, getting sloppy or falling so short you will never make the next base camp, the Lord is going to let you know about it." The Lord, Paul is telling us, really is partnering with us in our ascent.

It is the *attitude,* not the *altitude.* Paul is telling the Philippian Christians that it is not how far they have climbed but the focus of their hearts. Paul is talking to the *mature,* not to the perfect. These are the people who are already climbing and are focused on what is above, even though they may be several base camps below.

---

66   Phil. 3:13-17.

However, the *attitude* suggested from his biographical statement is indeed *radical*. It will be experienced only by those who are dying to live. Those who are living to salvage what they can out of life, with themselves at the center, simply cannot count what they are living for as loss. They can't consider their heartbreaking reversals as refuse or recycling material. Even when what is appropriately priceless is lost (a child, a mate, a best friend), we are not allowed to live the rest of our lives aimlessly.

If the resurrection of Christ infuses our perspective on life, our ability to cope with profound loss is also changed. We can be confident that he will eventually restore everything that needs to be restored. Our motivation must soar beyond whatever red carpet opportunities we have to the ultimate–resurrection life beginning now and lasting forever. This is what those who are dying to live will experience. Their gateway to this level of living requires that they share Christ's sufferings and be conformed to his death.

What then is of value to you? Are you tightly holding something that you won't be able to consider loss if you must? Suppose you are highly privileged among your peers and consistently stand on a pinnacle above then all. Are you prepared to consider all this loss and of little value compared to him and his high calling for you? Can you hold your position, power and privilege loosely?

If so, you are sharing the apostle's journey. You are dying to live in such a way that the very best of what is yet to come cannot be destroyed by the worst you may experience now. But the question for many of us is, "How? How does all this work? Do I have to create this reality? To what extent will God help me?" If our hearts are turned to the mountain pathways that snake above the red carpets of our lives, we can expect the Lord to lead us further. As Paul told the Philippian believers facing their own difficult challenges,

> And I am sure of this, that he who began a good work in you will bring it to completion at the day of Jesus Christ.[67]

The idea is, "What God started, he is big enough to finish." Don't say, "This lifestyle sounds great, but I don't have what it takes to make it up the mountain!" If God is calling you to the trail, he will be like a Sherpa to expertly guide you to the top of your Everest. If you are still struggling to get off your red carpet and find your way up the mountain, consider another confidence builder from Philippians.

> … work out your own salvation with fear and trembling, for it is God who works in you, both to will and to work for his good pleasure.[68]

How many times does God have to tell us in one short epistle that he is on our side–that we are not walking alone? Here we are told to work out the amazing dimensions of our calling because *God* is working both in our willingness and our practice as we attack the climb ahead.

A final note if you're thinking, "Okay, but I feel so alone. I love the Lord, but I can't *see* him. I just wish I had some *human* help!" With a smile Paul might reply, "It's interesting you brought this up." He focuses in Philippians on the support we are to receive from the community of Christians that surround us. Philippians

---

67   Phil. 1:6, ESV.
68   Phil, 2:12b-13, ESV.

is a relation-saturated book. Here is just one example of what Christ's community is to be like:

> So if there is any encouragement in Christ, any comfort from love, any participation in the Spirit, any affection and sympathy, complete my joy by being of the same mind, having the same love, being in full accord and of one mind. Do nothing from rivalry or conceit, but in humility count others more significant than yourselves. Let each of you look not only to his own interests, but also to the interests of others.[69]

Part of your struggle may be finding this community. Your first step is simply to understand that your journey is not intended to be an isolated marathon.

Paul has called us *not* to nihilism, loss for the sake of loss. He calls us not ultimately to death but to an incredible life through Christ Jesus the Lord. With a surging hope that soars far above any red carpet privilege, I say, "Go, and God be with you … and a whole lot of others be with you, too!"

DYING TO LIVE APPLICATION

Consider what you are valuing that may be hindering the climb to which you are called.

---

69   Phil. 2:1-4, ESV.

QUESTIONS FOR REFLECTION

What are your most significant red carpet privileges?

Why are they important to you? What do they do for you?

What substitute value would be substantial enough for you to give them up or at least hold them loosely?

CHAPTER 11

✠ ✠ ✠

Daniel: It's Not about You

DYING TO LIVE PRINCIPLE
Be clear about the real who *and the essential* what *of your life.*

"It's not about you," is the famous first line of Rick Warren's blockbuster best-seller, *The Purpose-Driven Life.* Warren continues, "We ask self-centered questions like What do I want to be? The purpose of your life is far greater than your own personal fulfillment, your peace of mind, or even your happiness. It's far greater than your family, your career, or even your wildest dreams and ambitions."[70] Unfortunately, many of us learn this lesson too late—or not at all.

And counsel that strokes and perpetuates this inborn selfishness is easy to find. Concerning our position and finances, we hear, "If you have made it to the top, don't lose what you've worked so hard to gain. Preserve your assets! Don't dissipate what you have accumulated. Control your own destiny. Don't let anybody else do it for you. It's *your* life. Don't let *anyone* tell you differently. You don't owe anybody *anything*. You did it yourself."

No doubt you are a committed Christian if you are persevering through this book. "You are preaching to the choir," you may be saying. "I know, deep down, that my life is not just

---

70   Rick, Warren. *The Purpose-Driven Life.* Grand Rapids, Mich.: Zondervan, 2007, 11.

about me." No doubt you mean this sincerely, but you and I most likely have more of the "I did it my way" attitude than either of us would like to admit.

This is understandable. Human existence can be so treacherous that instinctively we try to protect ourselves from its ravages. From almost any perspective, life is cruel and capricious. When our fear-driven efforts at self-preservation seemingly "pay off," we are, paradoxically, tempted to pride. I say "paradoxically" because sometimes there is no correlation between what we deserve and what we get. At times, the least deserving get the most. At other times, however, choice people receive special privilege and positions of power and influence. The question is, how do they handle it?

Daniel and his three friends attained a level far beyond their Babylonian associates. Today, we might label them as highly functional self-supporting emissaries embedded in a royal court. They had good reason to guard carefully what they had attained. They were ripped out of their native environment and plunked down in Nebuchadnezzar's court during his successful conquest of Jerusalem and Judah around 600 B.C. Nebuchadnezzar had wisely chosen to seed his administration with the brightest and best from the land he was conquering.

Daniel and his three friends—Shadrach, Meshach, and Abednego—have risen unexpectedly and spectacularly. Foreigners who crashed the inner circle of the court, however, could not expect a free pass. Envy and hatred were sure to bubble up against this Jewish foursome. Daniel's three associates were the first to face opposition, during Nebuchadnezzar's reign. Daniel was tested later, in the reign of Darius. For all their integrity, giftedness, and accomplishment, they had to learn a lesson that all of us face: It's not about us.

The lesson that Daniel and his three friends learned feels like a right cross to the jaw. A right cross is a great punch to deliver in boxing and a painful one to receive. The puncher delivers the blow to an opponent's head or body by extending his arm across his body, thereby gaining a great deal more leverage than merely lashing straight out. I remember blacking out for an instant when I received a blow like this.

I felt similarly during a recent Father's Day dinner. One of our married granddaughters (a former All-American athlete) and her husband gave me a sparkling gift. Indicative of their disciplines for spiritual growth, the gift was their memorization of Psalm 1 and a section from Isaiah. This was like strawberries and whipped cream on top of French vanilla ice cream for me.

Thinking of each member of my extended family, I was gripped with both pride and longing. "Lord," I prayed silently, "look after them. Don't let anything happen to them. Lead each to the knowledge of the Most High. May each be distinguished by what is really important."

Instead of that warm feeling you sometimes get after praying a good prayer, I felt a right cross to my soul. "Yes, of course it's all right to long for family members, to love them as best you can and wrap your arms around them," I sensed my heart answering me. "But, Charles, your family is not ultimately about you and, in the grand scheme of things, not even about them. It's about God, his interests, the divine program and his glory now and in the future."

Hananiah, Mishael and Azariah (the original, Hebrew names for Shadrach, Meshach and Abednego) hitchhiked on Daniel's astounding rise to fame and power. When Nebuchadnezzar insisted that the wise men in his court interpret one of his dreams, he refused to tell them the content of the dream. It was like a math teacher assigning a problem to be solved without revealing the numbers involved. Shocked and scared, the advisers told the king that no one except a divine being could do this.

Daniel, however, knows that it isn't about him. In a soaring prayer,[71] Daniel exalts God, celebrating his attributes and giving all the credit for what is to come to him. Then he speaks to Nebuchadnezzar, interpreting the dream and giving all the glory to God.

"As for you, O king, while on your bed your thoughts turned to what would take place in the future; and He who reveals mysteries has made known to you what will take place.

"But as for me, this mystery has not been revealed to me for any wisdom residing in me more than in any other living man, but for the purpose of making the interpretation known to the king, and that you may understand the thoughts of your mind."[72]

Although Nebuchadnezzar prostrated himself before Daniel, he got the message. "Surely your God is a God of gods and a Lord of kings and a revealer of mysteries, since you have been able to reveal this mystery."[73] Nebuchadnezzar's confused but improving theology seems to be better than what we might expect from a Babylonian ruler with minimal expo-

---

71   Daniel 2:20-23.
72   Daniel 2:29-30.
73   Daniel 2:47b.

sure to monotheism. Yet there are dangers ahead, for him, and for Shadrach, Meshach and Abednego.

After this professional success, Daniel was quickly promoted over the provincial area of Babylon and over all the wise men. He was at the top! Daniel then asked that his three close associates be appointed to posts as well. So they took over the administrative duties of the Babylonian prefect while he focused on responsibilities at the king's court.

However, riding in the wake of Daniel's career would have cost Shadrach, Meshach and Abednego their lives, apart from divine intervention. Nebuchadnezzar, misled by his own ego, required his subjects to worship his golden image.[74] With reckless fidelity to God, Daniel's three high-profile friends refused to comply, in effect challenging Nebuchadnezzar's supremacy. Now furious with them, Nebuchadnezzar prepared to throw them into a gigantic furnace.

Nebuchadnezzar, showing that Daniel's message had not yet sunk in, warned them, "Now if you are ready … to fall down and worship the image that I have made, very well. But if you do not worship, you will immediately be cast into the midst of a furnace of blazing fire; and what god is there who can deliver you out of my hands?"[75]

Daniel and Shadrach, Meshach and Abednego don't use the sophisticated rationale that we might employ. "We are the only pure witnesses to our God in the court," they might have said to themselves. "We can figure out a way to get around this and continue to serve the Lord at this highest level of Babylonian culture. There is no use squandering the opportunity we have

---

74   See Daniel 3 for the entire account.
75   Dan. 3:15.

been given. We can actually worship the one true God while faking respect for the image."

We sometimes use the same reasoning today: "My company is needed. We are a unique witness in the business community. I have a platform to reach high-level leaders in the business world, and all this would be lost if the company were moved off the scene. I would just be another Joe in my church and on the street. I need to do what is necessary to keep us viable and position us for how God will continue using us even if we bend a few rules here and there."

A young mother who had recently converted to the risen Christ but who was married to a radical Muslim could reason with impeccable logic: "I am the only Christian in my village. My children need me desperately, and I believe that my husband, who loves me, will eventually share my faith. I can compromise just enough to continue my new life with Christ and be a point of light in the darkness of Islam."

Walk with me now to a shallow grave, where a piece of her clothing sticks out of the ground, where her bones will lie until the resurrection. Look down the road a few years and see all of her children growing up as Muslims without ever finding the faith of their mother.

Yes, I am convinced that God can still use the business owner who feels that he must hold onto his business at all costs to be a servant of Christ in this realm. I likewise believe that the mother who made the necessary adjustments to continue as a daughter of Christ without being martyred can likewise be fruitful. However, in this chapter we are going beyond what is reasonable, sensible and logical. It's not about you. It's not about me. It's not about your business. It's not about your motherhood. It's not about your whatever it is.

Shadrach, Meshach and Abednego's response shows that they know all this.

"O Nebuchadnezzar, we do not need to give you an answer concerning this matter. "If it be so, our God whom we serve is able to deliver us from the furnace of blazing fire; and He will deliver us out of your hand, O king. "But even if He does not, let it be known to you, O king, that we are not going to serve your gods or worship the golden image that you have set up."[76]

In response to this godly defiance, the heat is increased sevenfold, killing the men who must get close enough to throw Shadrach, Meshach and Abednego into the furnace. The moving account that follows defies human explanation and makes fire-walking look like a pre-kindergarten exercise. An astounded Nebuchadnezzar comes as close as he dares to the furnace, exclaiming that while only three men were thrown in, now he sees a fourth: and "the appearance of the fourth is like a son of the gods!"[77]

In a state of shock, the king asks his intended victims to come of the furnace.

Then Nebuchadnezzar came near to the door of the furnace of blazing fire; he responded and said, "Shadrach, Meshach and Abednego, come out, you servants of the Most High God, and come here!" Then Shadrach, Meshach and Abednego came out of the midst of the fire. The satraps, the prefects, the governors and the king's high officials gathered around and saw in regard to these men that the fire had no effect on

76   Dan. 3:16b-18.
77   Dan. 3:25.

the bodies of these men nor was the hair of their head singed, nor were their trousers damaged, nor had the smell of fire even come upon them.

Nebuchadnezzar responded and said, "Blessed be the God of Shadrach, Meshach and Abednego, who has sent His angel and delivered His servants who put their trust in Him, violating the king's command, and yielded up their bodies so as not to serve or worship any god except their own God." Therefore I make a decree that any people, nation or tongue that speaks anything offensive against the God of Shadrach, Meshach and Abednego shall be torn limb from limb and their houses reduced to a rubbish heap, inasmuch as there is no other god who is able to deliver in this way." Then the king caused Shadrach, Meshach and Abednego to prosper in the province of Babylon.[78]

Nebuchadnezzar now has seen the God of Daniel and his three fellows do the impossible not once, but *twice*–interpret the impossible dream and reverse any conceivable natural law in the furnace. We are walking straight into the darkness that leads eventually to light. We are facing the stark truth that ultimately it's not about anything or anyone but God. The stakes are too high for anything else.

Yes, we know by reading this account that God delivered Shadrach, Meshach and Abednego from their furnace. But they didn't know the Lord was going to do this, which is why they said to Nebuchadnezzar, "Even if God does not...." On the front side of their experiences, they could not know what the outcome would be. The only thing they knew for sure was that what they

---

78   Daniel 3:26-30.

were facing was all about God. If they lived, that would be great. But if they died, that would work, too. We could conceivably face the same choice at some very dark crisis point in our lives.

Daniel's life or death test is yet ahead. Nebuchadnezzar has another dream.[79] He sees a tree that reaches to the sky. Not only birds lodge in it, but animals feed and shade themselves under it. The monstrous 145-foot banyan tree with over 300 animals carved into it on Disney World's Discovery Island in Orlando gives a faint idea of what this monster might have looked like. Shockingly, Nebuchadnezzar's vision calls for him to live and eat like an animal for seven years.

Daniel, called upon once more to interpret, is mortified and calls on the still-proud king to repent before it is too late: "O king, may my advice be pleasing to you: break away now from your sins by doing righteousness and from your iniquities by showing mercy to the poor, in case there may be a prolonging of your prosperity."[80]

But Nebuchadnezzar has not yet conquered his egomania. A year later, as he walks on the palace roof, he boasts, "Is this not Babylon the great, which I myself have built as a royal residence by the might of my power and for the glory of my majesty?"[81] Before he can finish his soliloquy, God's judgment falls like a lightning bolt: Nebuchadnezzar, who rules much of the known world, is brought low, forced to eat grass and live out in the elements, with his hair and fingernails becoming birdlike. His type of psychosis is not unknown in psychiatric literature.

Finally, the humbled king learns his lesson without losing his life.

---

79   See this account in Daniel 4.
80   Dan. 4:27.
81   Dan. 4:30.

"But at the end of that period, I, Nebuchadnezzar, raised my eyes toward heaven and my reason returned to me, and I blessed the Most High and praised and honored Him who lives forever;

For His dominion is an everlasting dominion,
And His kingdom endures from generation to generation.
"All the inhabitants of the earth are accounted as nothing,
But He does according to His will in the host of heaven
And among the inhabitants of earth;
And no one can ward off His hand
Or say to Him, 'What have You done?'

"At that time my reason returned to me. And my majesty and splendor were restored to me for the glory of my kingdom, and my counselors and my nobles began seeking me out; so I was reestablished in my sovereignty, and surpassing greatness was added to me.

"Now I, Nebuchadnezzar, praise, exalt and honor the King of heaven, for all His works are true and His ways just, and He is able to humble those who walk in pride."[82]

This confession is worthy of someone who is highly developed in the knowledge of God, both experientially and theologically. It comes about because Daniel and his three associates have lived the truth that it is not about them but God, whether this means death or life. When we live this way, others receive the opportunity to experience him—even pagans! Yet God is not through with Daniel. He has one more test, in his twilight years.

---

82   Dan. 4:34-37.

After Nebuchadnezzar and his inferior son, Belshazzar, have passed from the scene, Daniel, like cream, rises straight to the top under Darius the Mede. Daniel always seemed to be at the top of his game, and his peers hated him for it. This time they manipulate the king into an irreversible lose-lose situation. No one may pray to anyone but the sovereign king, under threat of being thrown to the lions. This presents a problem for Daniel, who is accustomed to praying openly.

Now when Daniel knew that the document was signed, he entered his house (now in his roof chamber he had windows open toward Jerusalem); and he continued kneeling on his knees three times a day, praying and giving thanks before his God, as he had been doing previously.[83]

I still remember my fright as a boy on my grandparent's farm when a rooster chased me, jumped up on my back and pecked at me. I was afraid of a chicken. Daniel did not fear lions.

Of course, he was readily found out by his enemies, and the king's hands were tied. Judgment was executed, and Daniel was cast into the lion's den. The king, broken-hearted, said feebly yet hopefully, "Your God whom you constantly serve will Himself deliver you."[84] Darius retired for a miserable, sleepless night and showed up at the lion's den as dawn broke.

When he had come near the den to Daniel, he cried out with a troubled voice. The king spoke and said to Daniel, "Daniel, servant of the living God, has your God, whom you constantly serve, been able to deliver you from the lions?" Then Daniel spoke to the king, "O king, live forever!

83 Dan. 6:10.
84 Dan. 6:16.

"My God sent His angel and shut the lions' mouths and they have not harmed me, inasmuch as I was found innocent before Him; and also toward you, O king, I have committed no crime."[85]

The result in the life of the king is predictable.

Then Darius the king wrote to all the peoples, nations and men of every language who were living in all the land: "May your peace abound! I make a decree that in all the dominion of my kingdom men are to fear and tremble before the God of Daniel;

For He is the living God and enduring forever,
And His kingdom is one which will not be destroyed,
And His dominion will be forever.
"He delivers and rescues and performs signs and wonders
In heaven and on earth,
Who has also delivered Daniel from the power of the lions."[86]

These great rulers were always able to move from the sold-out human instruments to God himself. These transplanted Jews in a Babylonian court realized it was not about them.

Have you broken your emotional connection between your heart and your position, place or status? Are you the CEO of a company you have sacrificed your life to build? If so, is God limited to using you on this platform or in this position? Or have you poured your life into your family? And would you be devastated if it did not turn out the way you hope? Are you protecting your life, or expending it for him? Since it's really not about you, would it be all right if he used you as food for lions? If you are like me, it is scary to ask these questions.

---

85   Dan. 6:20-22.
86   Dan. 6:25-27.

We can pray in dependent fashion: "Lord, we are hardly Daniels, Shadrachs, Meshachs, and Abednegos—not to mention many others throughout church history. Will you strengthen us in our feebleness and grip us with the knowledge that it is not about us? We know, in our heart of hearts, that it is ultimately about *you*. Help us, by your grace, to live that way. Amen."

DYING TO LIVE APPLICATION

If an emotional connection with your position, place, or status is tying you down, resolve to break it.

QUESTIONS FOR REFLECTION

What goes through your mind when hear, "It's not about you"? Do you resent this statement? Do you dismiss it as unrealistic religiosity … or does it resonate with you? Why?

Comment on your journey if you have begun to integrate this umbrella idea into your life.

Should you consider this as a call to help you get where you need to go in life? Is it possible that some readers have been stomped on or broken enough so that they will need to be first assured of their value?

CHAPTER 12

❊ ❊ ❊

Job: Destroyed by Disasters and Restored

DYING TO LIVE PRINCIPLE
God is worthy of your worship and love,
whatever your circumstances.

A friend and client of many years was sharing a meal with me at a North Shore hotel in Chicago. Suddenly the ambience was shattered when he raised both hands and exclaimed loudly, "I don't understand why God is dealing with me like this!"

Perhaps *you* have felt this way. Or maybe you are dealing with this kind of confusion and rage right now. God's people have asked *why* down through the ages while suffering unutterable pain, grief, rage or deeply embedded bitterness. We have developed a whole branch of theology, called theodicy, to attempt to justify God's seemingly inscrutable ways to man. Sometimes life seems monstrously unfair. Certainly Job was Exhibit A of this seeming unfairness.

Despite enjoying special and splendid blessings a few weeks earlier, Job reacted in complete hopelessness and rejection of his entire life.

After this Job opened his mouth and cursed the day of his birth. And Job said:

"Let the day perish on which I was born,
   and the night that said,

'A man is conceived.'
Let that day be darkness!
    May God above not seek it,
    nor light shine upon it.
Let gloom and deep darkness claim it.
    Let clouds dwell upon it;
    let the blackness of the day terrify it.
That night—let thick darkness seize it!
    Let it not rejoice among the days of the year;
    let it not come into the number of the months. …
Why did I not die at birth,
    come out from the womb and expire?"[87]

Job expresses his total desolation in the darkest of Hebrew poetry. He wishes that every vestige of his appearance on the planet could be wiped off the slate of human history.

In this same chapter he explores the *why* of life after it becomes pointless–when our worst fears and dread become actual experience.

"Why is light given to him who is in misery,
    and life to the bitter in soul,
who long for death, but it comes not,
    and dig for it more than for hidden treasures, …
For the thing that I fear comes upon me,
    and what I dread befalls me.[88]

The first question we are exploring with Job is *"Why?"* If we were praying this question, we could expand it to, "Lord, if

---

87   Job 3:1-6, 11, ESV.
88   Job 3:20-21, 25, ESV.

you are a wise and wonderful God, why do you permit mindless, random disasters to fall on people who are trying to live decent lives, let alone those who are your children through a covenant relationship? *Why?"*

In Job's case, we eventually come to both the *"why"* (Why did God let it happen?) and the *"what"* (What is he attempting to teach or reveal through Job?). Corrie Ten Boom's now famous statement from the horrors of the Nazi concentration camp hints at the story line of Job. "There is no pit so deep, that God's love is not deeper still."[89] Does the Book of Job reveal that God was beneath, beyond and above his tragedies? I believe it does. Let's see why.

Three supporting characters, Eliphaz the Temanite, Bildad the Shuhite and Zophar the Naamathite, tried valiantly to discover the *why* and the *what* of their friend's condition. They exceeded any standard of Western culture concerning friendship by simply sitting with him for seven days and nights before speaking.

> And when they saw him from a distance, they did not recognize him. And they raised their voices and wept, and they tore their robes and sprinkled dust on their heads toward heaven. And they sat with him on the ground seven days and seven nights, and no one spoke a word to him, for they saw that his suffering was very great.[90]

To this point, they have been magnificent. They set a permanent standard for relating to someone who is involved in a

---

89   Corrie Ten Boom quotes, GoodReads, http://www.goodreads.com/author/quotes/102203.Corrie_ten_Boom.

90   Job 2:12-13, ESV.

dying experience. Be present–really present. Share the person's grief, sorrow, pain or loss before engaging your mouth. We all should do so well. They fall short only when they begin to speak.

Their threefold cycle of responses to Job's situation and his grief-soaked replies (along with Elihu's eventual interjection) provide a riveting exposure to ancient literature in the canon of Scripture. However, the curtain is eventually drawn on all their human answers. Job's pitiful, broken, poignant retorts fall short. When God finally breaches the wall of silence and reminds those assembled of his infinitely superior wisdom, Job realizes that his assessment has utterly missed the mark, as he freely admits.

Then Job answered the LORD and said:

"I know that you can do all things,
    and that no purpose of yours can be thwarted.
'Who is this that hides counsel without knowledge?'
Therefore I have uttered what I did not understand,
    things too wonderful for me, which I did not know….
I had heard of you by the hearing of the ear,
    but now my eye sees you;
therefore I despise myself,
    and repent in dust and ashes."[91]

But this climactic chapter is not simply about the Lord's omnipotence and omniscience, as comforting as they might be to the one who is suffering. It is also about his love. God refers to Job as his "servant"–a beloved person in God's household. Beloved child and servant of God that you may be, do you remember this relationship in the midst of your troubles,

---

91   Job 42:1-3, 5-6, ESV.

or do you react to your circumstances in a way that fails to factor in who God really is to you and for you?

God's response to Eliphaz, Zophar and Bildad, however, is severe–much stronger than his corrective strategy with Job. However good their intentions were they failed fundamentally.

> After the LORD had spoken these words to Job, the LORD said to Eliphaz the Temanite: "My anger burns against you and against your two friends, for you have not spoken of me what is right, as my servant Job has. Now therefore take seven bulls and seven rams and go to my servant Job and offer up a burnt offering for yourselves. And my servant Job shall pray for you, for I will accept his prayer not to deal with you according to your folly. For you have not spoken of me what is right, as my servant Job has." So Eliphaz the Temanite and Bildad the Shuhite and Zophar the Naamathite went and did what the LORD had told them, and the LORD accepted Job's prayer.[92]

After Job has been rebuked, the Lord defends him before his three friends. Not only this, but Job becomes a priest to them. Their survival depends on his intervention. Then Job's fortunes are restored in astonishing fashion.

> And the LORD gave Job twice as much as he had before. Then came to him all his brothers and sisters and all who had known him before, and ate bread with him in his house. And they showed him sympathy and comforted him for all the evil that the LORD had

---

92   Job 42:7-9, ESV.

brought upon him. And each of them gave him a piece of money and a ring of gold.

And the LORD blessed the latter days of Job more than his beginning. And he had 14,000 sheep, 6,000 camels, 1,000 yoke of oxen, and 1,000 female donkeys. He had also seven sons and three daughters. And he called the name of the first daughter Jemimah, and the name of the second Keziah, and the name of the third Keren-happuch. And in all the land there were no women so beautiful as Job's daughters. And their father gave them an inheritance among their brothers. And after this Job lived 140 years, and saw his sons, and his sons' sons, four generations. And Job died, an old man, and full of days.[93]

Now that we have seen the real *end* of Job's story in this triumphant concluding portrait, we can return to the initial questions—*what* was God doing, and *why?* The *why* and *what* of your own experience may not be wrapped in such a neat package as Job's (but remember that Job had to walk through great darkness to arrive there). However, the principles and purpose embedded in his story have not changed from his time to ours.

The cosmic nature of the book and its evident early date indicate that Job's experience is not a small sideshow. Indeed, it is to be played out before the created intelligences of the universe, among whom Satan has his place. The stage is set in the first chapter.

Now there was a day when the sons of God came to present themselves before the LORD, and Satan also came among them. The LORD said to Satan, "From

93   Job 42:10b-17, ESV.

where have you come?" Satan answered the LORD and said, "From going to and fro on the earth, and from walking up and down on it." And the LORD said to Satan, "Have you considered my servant Job, that there is none like him on the earth, a blameless and upright man, who fears God and turns away from evil?" Then Satan answered the LORD and said, "Does Job fear God for no reason? Have you not put a hedge around him and his house and all that he has, on every side? You have blessed the work of his hands, and his possessions have increased in the land. But stretch out your hand and touch all that he has, and he will curse you to your face."[94]

The issue could hardly be clearer in Satan's challenge to God. Satan notes the obvious–Job is supremely blessed because of God's favor. The issue he is throwing in God's face is equally as blatant–Job (or by implication, anybody else in all of human history to come) will only continue to worship the Lord while receiving God's blessings. Take away the *sugar daddy* relationship, Satan sneers, and Job's loyalty will evaporate.

You have no doubt noticed, however, that it is *God* who precipitates this confrontation with Satan. God acts while Satan merely *re*acts. It is also clear that Job is the candidate selected from among every human being living at the time. "Have you considered my servant Job," God asks, "that there is none like him on the earth, a blameless and upright man, who fears God and turns away from evil?"

The principle that God is establishing at this early and strategic moment in history is still timely: *Whatever our circumstances, God is still worthy of our worship and love.* This is

---

94   Job 1:6-11, ESV.

true even when it appears that everything good, necessary and desirable for life has been lost and roiling waves carry us toward disaster or death.

The Lord is worthy when we stand at the pinnacle of life, privilege and blessing. He is also just as praiseworthy when we are experiencing a Job-like disaster. In fact, our circumstances don't dictate the merit of God. He is wonderful and to be worshiped with all of our hearts, whatever may be happening in our lives.

If you are going through a Job-like experience as you read this chapter–a child has died in a senseless automobile accident, cancer is draining your life away, or you are experiencing your most dreaded nightmare–Satan is *still* wrong. Our love for God cannot be dictated by the fleeting circumstances of our lives—whether on the height of ecstasy for a little while or in the darkest pit you have experienced (or somewhere in between).

Faced with this imperative, I instinctively pray, "Lord, have mercy on me and grant that I may be faithful to you and live consistently, whatever my circumstances. I will surely fail on my own." God is the sufficient answer in himself in any circumstance, whether or not we understand why we are going through it.

And sometimes we won't, and that's okay. Job didn't. After he has spoken in his sadness and devastation … raged and questioned … pleaded for enlightenment and a hearing with God . . . after Eliphaz, Zophar and Bildad had their say … after Elihu concludes the human analysis of Job's situation … God finally speaks! But note this: *God gives no reason or explanation!*

From our human perspective, we might expect that he owed Job an explanation. If anyone might have questioned

God, it would have been Job. Yet the Lord's first response to Job is not an answer, but a question.

> Then the LORD answered Job out of the whirlwind and said:

> "Who is this that darkens counsel by words without knowledge? Dress for action like a man;
>   I will question you, and you make it known to me.
> "Where were you when I laid the foundation of the earth?
>   Tell me, if you have understanding."[95]

The application for us is obvious. God does not owe us an explanation. God himself is a totally sufficient answer. His absoluteness in creation, in all his works, in his Person and in his character is sufficient, even though our hearts may be broken by circumstances we cannot understand.

When we, like Job, enter periods of terrifying darkness, the *what* and *why* of Job can instruct, stabilize and enlighten us. While the New Testament does not promise us the kind of restoration that Job received, our promised destiny in Christ makes our afflictions, whatever they are, light and trivial indeed.[96] Light from Job's life can shine, pierce and illuminate our darkest days.

So how did Job live differently after his encounter with God? How did he die to live? Probably like you, I love to revel in the wonderful reversal of fortune that God granted. If Job were a movie character, the credits would start to roll. But in real life, Job has 140 more years to live. I can't help but ask: Did Job simply go back to enjoying his doubled good fortune for the next

---

95   Job 38:1-4.
96   2 Cor. 4:17.

14 decades, or was something now different about him? How had he grown from the ordeal?

Of course, Job had *started* from a spiritual level few of us could even contemplate reaching. As I have said elsewhere, "He had achieved a spiritual state which was unexcelled in the world in his time and proved to be the one candidate to qualify for the grim task of having everything stripped away."[97]

Yet Job had not fully arrived. More spiritual surgery was required. Evelyn Underhill writes about this painful process:

> But still, in all this show and glitter of virtue, there is an unpurified bottom ... a selfishness which can no more enter into the Kingdom of Heaven than the grossness of flesh and blood can enter into it ... The self, then, has got to learn to cease to be its 'own centre and circumference': to make that final surrender which is the price of final peace. In the Dark Night the starved and tortured spirit learns through anguish ... to accept lovelessness for the sake of Love, Nothingness for the sake of All; dies without any sure promise of life, loses when it hardly hopes to find. It sees with amazement the most sure foundations of its transcendental life crumble beneath it, dwells in a darkness which seems to hold no promise of a dawn ... the last test of heroic detachment, of manliness, of spiritual courage.[98]

This deeply penetrating evaluation is implicit in the Book of Job. Even the best of us need God's painful discipline to

---

97   Charles Haley, *An Evangelical's Road Less Traveled* (Enumclaw, WA: Pleasant Word), 2009, 139.

98   Evelyn Underhill, *Mysticism: A Study in the Nature and Development of Man's Spiritual Consciousness* (London: Methuen & Co., Ltd., 1911; repr., New York: Adamant Media, 2004), 397.

grow. As the writer of Hebrews says, "For the moment all discipline seems painful rather than pleasant, but later it yields the peaceful fruit of righteousness to those who have been trained by it."[99]

Few who are reading this chapter, of course, would dare claim to have arrived at Job's pre-testing spiritual state. We do pray that we might emerge successfully, as Job did, from whatever trials we face to attain the stature ordained for us. This relevant and realistic prayer from Richard Foster and Gayle Beebe may help you frame your own.

Lord, we are a real mixture of motives when it comes to loving you. Would you please purify the stream of our loving, at least to the extent that we can stand it? Thank you. Amen.[100]

DYING TO LIVE APPLICATION
Ask God to purify your view of life and God to the extent you are able to stand it.

---

99   Heb. 12:11.
100   Foster and Beebe, *Longing for God*, 41; italics in original.

QUESTIONS FOR REFLECTION

Is the life of Job so extreme that you are unable to make a connection with your own?

What is the closest you have come to, or observed in another, a Job kind of experience?

You have been obliged to think about the unthinkable as you have viewed Job's life from beginning to end. Is there any reason to leave your life in God's hands even if it might include an element of disaster? Why would you do so and what might you expect?

✠ ✠ ✠

CHAPTER 13

Habakkuk: Dying to My National Expectations

DYING TO LIVE PRINCIPLE
*National expectations from your past
may not apply to your future.*

I read an article a couple of decades ago claiming that Americans lack a sense of tragedy because of a faulty, historically untested optimism. This is no longer the case. Something has definitely changed in the national consciousness.

Many pundits see America as a colossus in decline. A passel of opinion polls shows that many citizens believe the nation is on the wrong track. They see signs of moral, economic, and national decline everywhere they look. The exploding national debt, threats from Muslim extremists, weapons of mass destruction, moral decay, gridlocked politics, environmental catastrophe, and challenges from China and other undemocratic rivals seemingly have grown insurmountable. Many Americans, long known for their can-do spirit, fear that the country they love is collapsing before their eyes.

"Something's up," Peggy Noonan wrote in a column before the 9/11 attacks. "And deep down, where the body meets the soul, we are fearful. We fear, down so deep it hasn't even risen to the point of articulation, that with all our comforts and amusements, with all our toys and bells and whistles . . . we wonder if what we really have is . . . a first-class stateroom on the *Titanic*. Everything's wonderful, but a world is ending and we sense it."[101] In the wake of near daily reports of threats to our national security, that sense of fear has only intensified.

Today a litany of opinions appears regularly about why our nation's best days may be behind us. With strident voices clamoring for their rights, viewpoints, and agendas, sociologists ask whether we have enough national glue to hold our culture together. Historians wonder if Gibbon's *Decline and Fall of the Roman Empire* is happening all over again. After all, an unwise and uninformed majority can take a nation into oblivion–all it takes is a plurality.

We have heard that great nations last no more than 300 years on average. What about the USA, which is uncomfortably close to that span? Economists say that our soaring national debt is a time bomb. Who can stop the freight train when both major parties are frequently unable to discipline themselves and instead demonstrate an astounding lack of fiscal restraint? When a nation that has consistently provided us economic returns for our labors, stability versus anarchy, and a comfortable place to raise our families teeters on the brink of drastic change, we worry about the possibility of a dark and chaotic future.

We have just dialed Habakkuk's number! I am not a prophet–Habakkuk was. I remain dogmatically agnostic about the future and make no predictions about the fate of the United States. Some pundits see disaster just around the corner, while others predict that the nation will pull through

---

101   Peggy Noonan, "There Is No Time, There Will Be Time," *Forbes ASAP*, November 30, 1998, reposted September 18, 2001 by *The Wall Street Journal*, http://online.wsj.com/.

its current challenges, as it has done in the past. Hundreds of books, articles, Web entries and sermons address the fate of the United States–but the hand of history has not yet stamped the file folder of our country: *Closed*.

People (even the best of them) are frequently wrong, but the Bible never is. Habakkuk, one of its inspired writers, knew this first hand. Through this "minor" prophet's experience, we can understand not what the future may hold, but how we are to live regardless. This will involve, not surprisingly, a form of dying.

Habakkuk's prophecy was focused on the coming Babylonian captivity. In this small book God told Habakkuk that the brutal neo-Babylonians were about to overrun his beloved Israel. Three invasions and deportations then occurred between 606 through 586 B C. Daniel and his friends (the focus of Chapter 11) were taken to Babylon in the second deportation.

Unlike other prophets, Habakkuk had no external ministry to others. He did not speak to anyone. His only job was to "get it." His one task was to absorb the message God had for him. This meant he had to die to his national expectations, which were much stronger than ours. After all, we Americans *think* that God was involved in establishing America as a nation. Habakkuk *knew* this as fundamental truth. In fact, every Jew believed the same thing—that Israel was God's chosen people. We *believe* our democracy is distinctive and desirable. Habakkuk, however, *knew* that his nation was uniquely established as a theocracy (the direct, divine rule of God).

And the message that came to Habakkuk was direct and divine, unlike the current projections about the United States. Students of biblical prophecy, for their part, attempt to peer into the future to discover what might happen to our nation.

Many students of prophecy in their attempts to understand divine revelation about the future do not see the United States playing any significant role in world events. Why not? They conclude that America will have passed from the scene as a major player!

Habakkuk has one of the most obvious structures of any book of the Bible. In the first few verses, the author complains about the sad condition of the country and comes close to accusing the Lord of not paying attention or of being too lax. God's response in Chapter 1 blows him away. The Lord says he is going to send the neo-Babylonians, a people more wicked than Israel, to execute his judgment. "Lord, this can't be!" a panicked Habakkuk hastily replies. "Using people like that would violate your character!"

In his stunned state, in Chapter 2 Habakkuk takes a solitary sojourn while waiting for God to give him the insight he desperately needs. God's response is powerfully to the point. "Write the vision I am giving you. Record it plainly so that people can run with it." The rest of the chapter describes the wicked nation (the Babylonians) that God will use as his instrument of judgment—and then destroy!

Chapter 3 records Habakkuk's journey to receive and internalize this message. He rises triumphantly in his own soul from the initial desolation to the spectacular conclusion.

But before we get there, let's return to the beginning for further insights. While Habakkuk's prayer at the outset of his book is a little bolder and brash than our national praying, it is not entirely different. You have no doubt grieved in your prayers for the United States (or whatever country you call home). "Lord, what has happened to our country? Have mercy on us. Bring revival. Turn us away as a nation from our road to destruction, disaster and death."

Habakkuk takes this a step further when he prays,

O LORD, how long shall I cry for help,
 and you will not hear?
Or cry to you "Violence!"
 and you will not save?
Why do you make me see iniquity,
 and why do you idly look at wrong?
Destruction and violence are before me;
 strife and contention arise.[102]

As the prophet soon finds out, this is a dangerous prayer. God's answer has an impact similar to what we would feel were we to learn that radical Muslims or old line communists would soon take over. God's answer, that the hated and feared neo-Babylonians are going to invade, is an appalling development for which Habakkuk is totally unprepared.

In the third and final chapter, however, the prophet successfully integrates this message into his life but ends with an attitude change that is seldom, if ever, duplicated in the Bible: "yet I will rejoice in the LORD; I will take joy in the God of my salvation."

How did Habakkuk get here? It is a breathtaking journey, and we will attempt very briefly to travel it with him. In the first two verses of his final chapter, he acknowledges the fearsomeness of the message but does not stop there. In fact, he calls out to the Lord.

O LORD, revive Your work in the midst of the years,
In the midst of the years make it known;
In wrath remember mercy.[103]

---

102   Habakkuk 1:2-3, ESV.
103   Habakkuk 3:2b.

For those of us who similarly may be grief-stricken over current events, go ahead and pray this prayer. Be reckless because of the greatness of God. Be bold. God's hands are not tied by a nation's downfall. He is able to bring life-giving revival and a sunrise of mercy even in a time of national disaster. Pray a big prayer, as Habakkuk did!

Three *selah*s, like those in the Psalms, punctuate the prophet's bold praying. They tell us not to rush over this newfound perspective of the prophet. "Be there and make sure you get it," is the idea. Habakkuk continues with a radiant verbal vision of God's glory. God is incomprehensibly, incomparably and consistently great, glorious and good! This is a strong place to start and a foundation on which to pray his revival prayer.

We come to the next section of Habakkuk's prayer.

God came from Teman,
  and the Holy One from Mount Paran.
His splendor covered the heavens,
  and the earth was full of his praise.

Selah

His brightness was like the light;
  rays flashed from his hand;
  and there he veiled his power.
Before him went pestilence,
  and plague followed at his heels.
He stood and measured the earth;
  he looked and shook the nations;
then the eternal mountains were scattered;
  the everlasting hills sank low.
  His were the everlasting ways.

I saw the tents of Cushan in affliction;
　the curtains of the land of Midian did tremble.
Was your wrath against the rivers, O LORD?
　Was your anger against the rivers,
　or your indignation against the sea,
when you rode on your horses,
　on your chariot of salvation?
You stripped the sheath from your bow,
　calling for many arrows.

Selah

　You split the earth with rivers.
The mountains saw you and writhed;
　the raging waters swept on;
the deep gave forth its voice;
　it lifted its hands on high.
The sun and moon stood still in their place
　at the light of your arrows as they sped,
　at the flash of your glittering spear.
You marched through the earth in fury;
　you threshed the nations in anger.
You went out for the salvation of your people,
　for the salvation of your anointed.
You crushed the head of the house of the wicked,
　laying him bare from thigh to neck.

Selah

You pierced with his own arrows the heads of his warriors,
　who came like a whirlwind to scatter me,
　rejoicing as if to devour the poor in secret.

You trampled the sea with your horses,
    the surging of mighty waters.[104]

Harold Willmington comments succinctly and significantly on this section:

> Throughout Israel's history–at the Exodus, in the wilderness, at the Jordan, during the days of Joshua– God had delivered them by his mighty power, and his power was fearsome to behold! ... Just as God delivered his people from the Red Sea, so he would deliver them from the flood of the Chaldeans. Once again, however, God's judgment was presented as nothing to be taken lightly ... The benefit of prayer is not that it changes God, but that it changes the one who prays![105]

Looking back, we can understand that Habukkuk's prayer is brilliant. God wins out in human history. His manifested works are matchless. They are wonderful, right and perfectly dependable over the long term, even though we may see them through temporary grief, heartbreak and desolation. This is an easy thing to say; it is another thing entirely to live. But that's why we are called to die to live. That's what Habakkuk did.

If we learn his lesson, we can look at the possibility of national disaster squarely and realistically. Like Habakkuk, we can ascend to a height that we would never have attained previously. God can make our feet like the deer's, allowing us to tread on our high places. We don't need to be in denial about the terrifying events that may come upon us and our nation. Here is the prayer he is now ready to pray and turn over to the choir director—one that we need to be able to pray, too:

104   Hab. 3:3-15, ESV.

105   Willmington, *Willmington's Bible Handbook*, 491-92.

I hear, and my body trembles;
  my lips quiver at the sound;
rottenness enters into my bones;
  my legs tremble beneath me.
Yet I will quietly wait for the day of trouble
  to come upon people who invade us.
  Though the fig tree should not blossom,
  nor fruit be on the vines,
the produce of the olive fail
  and the fields yield no food,
the flock be cut off from the fold
  and there be no herd in the stalls,
yet I will rejoice in the LORD;
  I will take joy in the God of my salvation.
GOD, the Lord, is my strength;
  he makes my feet like the deer's;
  he makes me tread on my high places.[106]

Reflecting upon this prayer, you can no longer feel sorry for Habakkuk. He has been vaulted beyond his immediate circumstances, however dire, and is breathing the pure air of spiritual triumph. No doubt you want the same kind of victory for yourself.

This victory didn't come easily for Habakkuk, however. It was preceded by trauma. He got the trembles inwardly, his lips quivered like someone who has been traumatized and will momentarily break out into sobs. Rather than curling up into an emotional fetal position, the prophet's next step is simply to wait for the perspective he so desperately needs. Habakkuk contemplates the collapse of an agrarian economy, akin to today's stock market falling to 10 instead of 10,000.

---

106   Hab. 3:16-19, ESV.

It is only at this point, when he honestly contemplates the destruction of his beloved nation, that Habakkuk is ready to soar to such great heights with the word, *"yet."* Habakkuk does not see himself as just surviving but as *exulting.* Habakkuk does more than endure. He rejoices in the God he has come to know at a much deeper level than when he had the foolish brashness to claim at the outset that God was not doing his job.

Now he understands that the Lord is more than Someone who guarantees the continuity of his nation. God's plans are much bigger than ours. Yes, the days ahead for Habakkuk may be very dangerous. However, Habakkuk expects to be like a deer walking at the top of a 3,000-foot precipice, where a misstep means a few pieces of hair and bones at the bottom. He will navigate these perilous times–not simply *somehow,* but with a graced ability that was inconceivable when he first cried out to the Lord. Habakkuk will be like the deer that leaps with confident agility in the most dangerous mountain terrain.

Getting hold of Habakkuk's message has not been easy for me, and I am still in process. I love my country and dread to think about the tragic events which may be ahead. Love of country, up to a point, is natural and good. Yet patriotism has its limits. Christians are called to a higher allegiance, trusting the compassionate and almighty God who holds the fate of nations, including ours, in his hands. In the days ahead, we and those we influence may need this perspective as much as Habakkuk did.

Are you willing to die a necessary but painful death to *whatever* national expectations you might have? Are you aware of how much others may need what you are learning through your own temporary grief? If so, let Habakkuk lead the way.

His counsel has been tested for 2,500 years. It may be more relevant and timely than we could ever have imagined.

DYING TO LIVE APPLICATION

Relinquish your own national expectations to the plan and purposes of God no matter how confusing or troubling this might be.

QUESTIONS FOR REFLECTION

How deeply is your Christian faith linked to life in a free and democratic society?

Do you need to re-evaluate the mixing of these two perspectives?

As a Jew who had only known what it was like to live in the most favored nation in the world, Habakkuk was compelled to lay aside all his national assumptions. How might this severe instruction of God to Habakkuk be timely for Americans or citizens of other nations today?

CHAPTER 14

☒ ☒ ☒

Moses: Learning to Die after Extreme Living and Leadership

DYING TO LIVE PRINCIPLE
Hold onto your place with an open hand.

I am pained these days when I turn on the radio and hear the voice of a particular leader. He founded one of the great Christian radio networks, which has blessed uncounted thousands in the U.S. and abroad. Later in life, he adopted a point of view so strange that I cannot fathom it. This leader, no doubt a great and godly man who has a wonderful knowledge of Scripture, claims that the church in its local form is no longer valid and that radio (and TV as well, I suppose) is the only proper church venue today. More recently, he has attempted to place a date on the Lord's second coming.

I think about the outstanding staff he assembled and the embarrassment they must feel. Clearly this man, who started so well, stayed on too long. How about the rest of us in leadership? Are we able to die to what we have launched and step aside for someone else?

The time for Moses' exit came after one of the greatest careers in history. The human author of the Pentateuch, Moses has multitudes of admirers among the world's three great monotheistic religions. Jews revere him as the lawgiver.

Muslims exalt him as a noble prophet. Christians honor him as one of the great leaders of the Old Testament.

If any person's life was under the providential care of God, it was that of Moses. Beyond all odds, he becomes an adopted grandson of Pharoah, after his daughter rescues him in his wicker basket from the Nile. Moses' career is timeless, a chronicle of a strategic time in the spiritual history of mankind.

Moses was extremely well prepared to assume his role. Born into an environment in which Jewish male babies were to be exterminated, he was unexpectedly prepared by his own family for life in the royal Egyptian household. When Moses eventually stood before Pharaoh, he knew the language, culture, religion, mythology and life of the royal court.

Do you see any parallels to your own (much less spectacular) career? Moses began his life as a *preserved* person. He was the *drawn out one*–plucked out of the Nile. His entire career evidenced *preparation*. It is not surprising, then, that he *performed* wonderfully during his tenure as the leader of God's people. How has God prepared *you* for your own time in history?

Moses interacted with God as no man ever had. This relationship was so intense that at one point his face radiated a residual glory from being in the presence of the Most Holy. A large chunk of Exodus focuses on Moses meeting God on Sinai as the people's representative and intermediary.

Moses' leadership is both breathtaking and moving. Moses strides across the landscape of the Pentateuch. In Leviticus, he presides over the religious laws. He leads the wanderings of the people in the Sinai Desert until the unbelieving generation passes from the scene. He rises to profound heights in the second giving of the law in Deuteronomy. He delivers that law to the new generation as it waits on the plains of Moab before crossing the Jordan to take possession of the land.

Yet, like us, Moses had to grow into his position. At the dawn of his calling, perhaps Moses' inborn impetuousness or an over-acquaintance with the privilege of power prompted him to kill an Egyptian who had bullied a fellow Jew. Years in the silent Sinai wilderness followed, when this shepherd was called into relationship with the self-revealing God. Moses eventually stood alone between this God and the oft-difficult people he was called to lead.

Wilderness experiences change us all. Moses' impetuousness and hot temper were moderated. His people, the Israelites, smoothed his rough edges through their incessant complaining and nearly constant unfaithfulness. During one incident, Moses passed a test of patience.

> Then all the congregation of the sons of Israel journeyed by stages from the wilderness of Sin, according to the command of the LORD, and camped at Rephidim, and there was no water for the people to drink. Therefore the people quarreled with Moses and said, "Give us water that we may drink." And Moses said to them, "Why do you quarrel with me? Why do you test the LORD?" But the people thirsted there for water; and they grumbled against Moses and said, "Why, now, have you brought us up from Egypt, to kill us and our children and our livestock with thirst?"[107]

Having grown more mature, Moses didn't take matters into his own hands but instead reflected the people's grumbling back to the Lord. Then God directed Moses to strike the rock

---

107   Exod. 17:1-3.

of Horeb. The man of God complied, and a spontaneous river cascaded forth in a previously desolate place. According to the Apostle Paul, the rock was a type of Christ, who was broken so that we could drink the water of eternal life.[108]

Years later, it was *deja vu* all over again. There was no water for the congregation, and the people assembled against Moses and Aaron.

> The people thus contended with Moses and spoke, saying, "If only we had perished when our brothers perished before the LORD!" "Why then have you brought the LORD'S assembly into this wilderness, for us and our beasts to die here? "Why have you made us come up from Egypt, to bring us in to this wretched place? It is not a place of grain or figs or vines or pomegranates, nor is there water to drink."[109]

Look at the passage. After all this time, the people of Israel aren't any more developed in journeying with Moses and God than they had been at first. Sadly, Moses fails, too. At this point, after sojourning for so long in the desert, Moses is tired. He is aging. His emotional and spiritual defenses are worn down.

Much earlier, before he became the seasoned leader of the people, he had killed an Egyptian. This time, the hot-tempered leader violated a sacred typology, with severe consequences. According to Numbers 20:6-11, God this time instructed his representative to speak to the rock, but Moses struck it again, not once, but twice. Three thousand years in the future, Jesus the Messiah would eventually die after being struck once for all time and eternity on the Cross. As a result, God's grace is still

---

108   1 Cor. 10:4.
109   Num. 20:3-5.

surging from his sacrifice. Striking the rock twice symbolized a monstrous, blasphemous impossibility–Jesus needing to die as the Lamb of God twice!

Not totally unlike a contestant on *American Idol* or *The Apprentice*, Moses fails to make the cut. As Donald Trump might say, "You're fired!" This leader, one of the greatest of all time, would not make it into the Promised Land.[110] Now the book on Moses the extraordinary man of God would be closed.

It is not because he has grown too feeble to continue. Yes, he is 120 years old, but his vigor and physical senses have remained. It was God's choice and his alone. God instructs this giant of history to hand over leadership of the nation to his young protégé, Joshua.[111] Then God shows Moses the land that he will never enter.

> Now Moses went up from the plains of Moab to Mount Nebo, to the top of Pisgah, which is opposite Jericho and the LORD showed him all the land, Gilead as far as Dan, and all Naphtali and the land of Ephraim and Manasseh, and all the land of Judah as far as the western sea, and the Negev and the plain in the valley of Jericho, the city of palm trees, as far as Zoar. Then the LORD said to him, "This is the land which I swore to Abraham, Isaac, and Jacob, saying, 'I will give it to your descendants'; I have let you see it with your eyes, but you shall not go over there." So Moses the servant of the LORD died there in the land of Moab, according to the word of the LORD. And He buried him in the valley

---

110   Num. 27:12-14.
111   Deut. 31:14-15.

in the land of Moab, opposite Beth-peor; but no man knows his burial place to this day.[112]

None of us could summon enough superlatives to do justice to Moses' life and career. Yet he was commanded to step aside. The question we must ask is whether *any* leader is indispensable or irreplaceable. The obvious answer, straight from the life of Moses, is "No!" In God's economy and wisdom, *any* leader is replaceable, even Moses. Leaders, like everyone else, must die to their own sense of indispensability and duty. If not, they become their own little god and risk seeing their leadership role ripped from their dying hand.

We use the words such as *succession* or *exit strategy* today. How well did Moses handle his own succession? What do you think his first thought was after God notified him that he would be barred from entering the land? Here is what Moses cried out so nobly:

"May the LORD, the God of the spirits of all flesh, appoint a man over the congregation, who will go out and come in before them, and who will lead them out and bring them in, so that the congregation of the LORD will not be like sheep which have no shepherd."[113]

Moses' thoughts were only for the people he had led, not for himself. Would you have done so well? Would I? There is only one way to find out.

Leader, you are not indispensable. You have given much, and maybe you have even been recognized for it. But how will your time of leadership end? Are you willing to pass the baton?

---

112   Deut. 34:1-6.
113   Num. 27:16-17.

Perhaps your final act of greatness will be to hand it over to God. Will you bring your "A game" to your end game?

Exit strategies are not just for those of us privileged to lead organizations, of course. Mothers who rise to great heights and lead their families into generations of wholeness and productivity must be willing to lay aside this most sacred task. Sunday school teachers who build godliness and love into the lives of their students week after week must be willing to walk away alone and leave the results to God. It makes no difference whether you are a great pastor, CEO, coach, school principal, manager of a department that is critical to the success of a company, president of a university or seminary, an elected official who serves at a high level, the founder of a prestigious magazine, a woman who founded and runs the best day care center in town or a father who has devoted his life to his family and is now a feeble great-grandfather. All of us have absolute and final accountability to God, who determines not only the course of our vocations but also their ending.

Part of dying to live as a leader involves a final act of giving over to God what was his all along—your role that you managed well and honorably but only for a little while. Now, go back and look at Moses in his final moments all over again. Suppose he would have clutched the place, prerogative and performance that positioned him as one of history's greatest leaders. We might have seen a tragic precursor of Saul's pathetic clutching of the throne when David was called to succeed him. But as it was, Moses was as heroic in finally dying to his sacred leadership role for the ages as he was in performing it.

Sit with Moses at this stage of his life and leadership. Envision yourself in the same place somewhere down the road. Now get up, leave that place, and be God's servant leader, someone who stands above small-hearted frontrunners who fail to appreciate their status for what it is–fleeting. Serve well in the knowledge that every day you live out your sacred place and position, you are dying to live. This is the pathway to life at its best, not only for you, but also for those whom you serve.

DYING TO LIVE APPLICATION

Be willing to relinquish the role that has distinguished your life and support your successor.

QUESTIONS FOR REFLECTION

How can someone with a large leadership platform find value in recognizing that his or her career is limited both in time and breadth?

Would it take the edge off your performance if you were prepared to leave this function behind?

What is the most important thing to keep in mind as you approach the end of your leadership career?

CHAPTER 15

❦ ❦ ❦

Joseph and the Dungeon

DYING TO LIVE PRINCIPLE
See beyond your dungeon.

Sixty-nine days and eight hours after 700,000 tons of rubble collapsed in the San Jose Mine near Copiano, Chile, the 33rd and final miner ascended through 2,000 feet of rock to freedom. The world held its collective breath because no miners had ever survived so deep a collapse. Then it let out a concerted cheer when the men were freed. Does this famous incident remind you of any type of dungeon experience you have endured?

Think back to your own dark time in the dungeon. You were trapped. There was no way out. You could only hope against hope that you would see daylight again. Life had collapsed on top of you. How could you ever be rescued?

Whether you are recalling an incident from your own life or some event like the 2010 Chilean mine collapse, we can all identify with the dungeon episodes of life. In these seasons of being buried alive, the concept of dying to live comes to us with the clarity of a shaft of light illuminating the recesses of a cramped, underground chamber.

When Joseph was imprisoned in his own dungeon, life had surely collapsed on him. He was the youngest and most favored son of his doting and wealthy father, Jacob. For some reason known only to God, he was given a green light for the rest of his life in a vision just for him. He was destined to reign supreme over his siblings and even his parents.[114]

It all ended suddenly. When Jacob sent Joseph to check on his other sons and on the flocks they were shepherding, his brothers grabbed the young man. They debated about killing him out of jealousy but instead permitted him to be sold to traders who were on their way to Egypt.

Joseph's superior ability surfaced when he was bought by Potiphar and placed over the Egyptian official's affairs. When Joseph refused to be seduced by his wife, however, she accused him of violating her. Potiphar avoided having him executed but had him thrown into a dungeon instead.

At least the 33 miners had the world cheering for them, families waiting to embrace them and a country mobilized behind the unparalleled rescued attempt. But Joseph had no such audience. This man, full of so much promise, was utterly alone. He not only had lost his family, his own brothers were the ones who had sold him into slavery.

Your time in the dungeon might be quite minor compared with Joseph's. But have you ever thought about how it has affected your life? Psychologists warn that time in a dungeon, or perhaps a Chilean mine, can have long-lasting effects on us, even when we seem to have emerged unscathed. We can surmise that Joseph's deadly dungeon time was a critical and pivotal point for the rest of his life. How do we know? Fascinatingly enough, the commentary that leads to this conclusion comes in a few short words in a completely different section of the Bible.

---

114   See Genesis 37.

When [God] summoned a famine on the land
   and broke all supply of bread,
he had sent a man ahead of them,
   Joseph, who was sold as a slave.
His feet were hurt with fetters;
   his neck was put in a collar of iron;
until what he had said came to pass,
   the word of the LORD tested him.[115]

This commentary in the Psalms will illuminate why Joseph's deadly dungeon experience was so critical—and why *ours* is as well. A dungeon experience involves being forced into a frighteningly restricted place. With trust in the God who sometimes allows us to go into such situations, we have the prospect of eventually living on an elevated plane.

This passage in Psalms will enable us to answer a number of critical questions about Jospeh's dungeon experience—and ours:

- *What* was going on with Joseph in his deadly dungeon?
- *How* did it prepare him for his stratospheric life ahead?
- *Does* Joseph's shift in an Egyptian prison provide an important life lesson for us today?
- *What* is that lesson?

Joseph had two choices while he sat shackled, his feet in fetters. One was to accept the dark reality in which he found himself as the *only* reality. The other was to look beyond it to *God's* reality. Which would he choose? Which would *we* choose?

---

115   Psa. 105:16-19, ESV.

A deadly dungeon experience helps us separate our daily experience from essential reality, which transcends what we experience in space and time. Alexander Solzhenitsyn, a survivor of the Soviet Gulag, discovered that his time in darkness shed light on his own evil heart:

> It has granted me to carry away from my prison years on my bent back, which nearly broke beneath its load, this essential experience: *how* a human being becomes evil and *how* good. In the intoxication of my youthful successes I had felt myself to be infallible, and I was therefore cruel. In the surfeit of power I was a murderer, and an oppressor. In my most evil moments I was convinced that I was doing good, and I was well supplied with systematic arguments. And it was only when I lay there on rotting prison straw that I sensed within myself the first strivings of good. Gradually it was disclosed to me that the line separating good and evil passes not through states, nor between classes, nor between political parties either—but right through every human heart—and then all human hearts... And even within hearts overwhelmed by evil, one small bridgehead of good is retained. And even in the best of all hearts, there remains... an unuprooted small corner of evil.[116]

In the dark keep of an extended prison incident, some might say we are limited to seeing only the four walls in the

---

116   From Alexander Solzhenitsyn, *The Gulag Archipelago Two* (Harper and Row, New York, 1975), pp. 615-616, quoted in Seraphim Rose, "Alexander Solzhenitsyn and the Gulag," OrthodoxPhotos.com, http://www.orthodoxphotos.com/readings/seraphim/revival/alexander.shtml.

dim light of our cell. That is untrue! Joseph's experience shows that we have the opportunity to see a million miles away.

Why does the text of the psalm say that *the word of the LORD tested him*? When Joseph passes this test, why then is he prepared for a subsequent spectacular life chapter that is an essential part of God's redemptive plan?

The word of the LORD tested him. While Joseph sat in almost unspeakable desolation in his shackles, his circumstances were unbearably real. Remember, the word of God in his vision said that he would be supreme in his family. For some reason, all its members would bow to him.

The view from his prison cell certainly provided no corroborating evidence of this. From a human point of view, there was almost no chance he would ever see his family again, let alone reign over them. Instead of being elevated to whatever supremacy the vision pointed to, he was a slave, and sitting in an Egyptian dungeon, from which he might never be freed.

Yet, *the word of the LORD tested him.* "Joseph," he might have asked himself, "are you going to believe your all too real circumstances, or are you going to believe God and what he told you?" What an almost cruel test for a young man who had so recently paraded around in a special coat, which had set him apart as the favored one among his brothers? Joseph no doubt received the best piece of meat when they ate, the first choice whenever possible. How could such a pampered young man ever withstand this kind of test?

And yet he did! At university, one of my professors labeled Joseph's story one of the most outstanding in all of literature, and of course it is. You will be gripped as you read it starting in Genesis 37 and in the following chapters.

In one sense, Joseph's chronicle could easily have become fodder for a Greek tragedy—if he had failed. Yet he did not.

Through an incredible set of circumstances, he gets out of prison and eventually meets his brothers, who come as virtual beggars at the command of Jacob to look for an Egyptian handout. They have no way of knowing that the great official before whom they grovel is the brother whom they had sold into slavery so many years before.

Even here we see that we are part of a story larger than our own. Joseph's narrative in the latter chapters of Genesis is interrupted repeatedly by that of his family. *Joseph is one of the greatest examples in all the Bible of how personal, family and professional life can all come together in a seamless whole.*

Since Joseph has passed his deadly dungeon test, he is ready *personally* when his brothers stand before him in unadulterated obeisance. Joseph, now a great man, refuses to give in to any bitterness, blind rage, or brutal instincts. Joseph could have wiped these jealous plotters out with a single gesture— but he didn't.

Instead, after Joseph flees to weep uncontrollably in another room, he eventually reveals himself to them in the Egyptian court. In this wonderful episode Joseph is modeling in a pagan environment the height of godliness. Even Pharaoh's household became aware of this riveting drama.

Having risen to heights seldom scaled personally after his time in the dungeon, Joseph is ready to address the *family issues* that can no longer be avoided. Here is the way it finally plays out.

> Then Joseph could not control himself before all those who stood by him. He cried, "Make everyone go out from me." So no one stayed with him when Joseph made himself known to his brothers. And he wept aloud, so that the Egyptians heard it, and the household

of Pharaoh heard it. And Joseph said to his brothers, "I am Joseph! Is my father still alive?" But his brothers could not answer him, for they were dismayed at his presence.

So Joseph said to his brothers, "Come near to me, please." And they came near. And he said, "I am your brother, Joseph, whom you sold into Egypt. And now do not be distressed or angry with yourselves because you sold me here, for God sent me before you to preserve life. For the famine has been in the land these two years, and there are yet five years in which there will be neither plowing nor harvest. And God sent me before you to preserve for you a remnant on earth, and to keep alive for you many survivors. So it was not you who sent me here, but God. He has made me a father to Pharaoh, and lord of all his house and ruler over all the land of Egypt. Hurry and go up to my father and say to him, 'Thus says your son Joseph, God has made me lord of all Egypt. Come down to me; do not tarry. You shall dwell in the land of Goshen, and you shall be near me, you and your children and your children's children, and your flocks, your herds, and all that you have. There I will provide for you, for there are yet five years of famine to come, so that you and your household, and all that you have, do not come to poverty.' And now your eyes see, and the eyes of my brother Benjamin see, that it is my mouth that speaks to you. You must tell my father of all my honor in Egypt, and of all that you have seen. Hurry and bring my father down here." Then he fell upon his brother Benjamin's neck and wept, and Benjamin wept upon his neck. And he kissed all his brothers and wept upon them. After that his brothers talked with him.

When the report was heard in Pharaoh's house, "Joseph's brothers have come," it pleased Pharaoh and his servants.[117]

To say this account is moving doesn't do it justice. Setting aside for a moment its intense emotions and settling for objectivity, it is obvious that Joseph saw his family, and more specifically, his brothers, in a much bigger light than the terrible personal wounds they had inflicted on him.

Joseph's words at their moment of maximum vulnerability and self-knowledge acknowledge their evil deeds but immediately place them in the larger context of God's plan.

And now do not be distressed or angry with yourselves because you sold me here, for God sent me before you to preserve life. For the famine has been in the land these two years, and there are yet five years in which there will be neither plowing nor harvest. And God sent me before you to preserve for you a remnant on earth, and to keep alive for you many survivors. So it was not you who sent me here, but God.

Can Joseph actually be telling his evil and vengeful brothers that in their terrible act they were de facto servants of God? Instead of facing the death sentence they expected, they are face to face with a forgiving brother, one who could have disposed of them as easily as if he were swatting a fly.

Most of us become wounded in our families in one way or another. I can't count the number of stories I have heard that

---

117   Gen. 45:1-16, ESV.

testify to this unfortunate reality. But Joseph shows that we can rise above whatever familial injustices we have experienced. When we do, we can eventually bring healing that will help our family members rise to the potential God has for them. It is a lofty calling, but the price is often high.

Joseph's time in a deadly dungeon also has *professional* implications. It is quite clear from the account in Genesis that something very big is occurring. Israel is saved from a famine before the nation eventually returns to the Promised Land. We see this when we flip ahead to the prophet Hosea:

> When Israel was a child, I loved him,
> and out of Egypt I called my son.[118]

Eventually Israel is called to return to Canaan. If that were not enough, the Gospel of Matthew places Joseph's actions in an even grander context, with another Joseph involved.

> And [Joseph] rose and took the child and his mother by night and departed to Egypt and remained there until the death of Herod. This was to fulfill what the Lord had spoken by the prophet, "Out of Egypt I called my son."[119]

This is a double reference to both the Savior and the nation of Israel, who both came "out of Egypt." This is the big picture that was coming into focus with Joseph and his brothers. God was using Joseph to prepare a place for his extended family to incubate into a nation. This is the family who had received the Abrahamic Covenant. The Savior and Holy Scripture were to come from this nation. One could say that this confrontation

---

118   Hos. 11:1, ESV.
119   Matt. 2:14-15, ESV.

between Joseph and his brothers involved us as well. Joseph understood what was really going on.

So then, *professionally,* what had transpired? Joseph knew that his near miraculous rise to fame, power and influence was not primarily for his personal fulfillment and vindication. Providentially, he was given a *professional* platform to fulfill a much larger plan and program. This, by the way, is normative in the Bible. Great servants of God do not receive their prominent roles primarily for their own benefit, pleasure or fulfillment. They walk across the stage of history and facilitate the unfolding of the divine design.

So we see that *the word of the LORD tested* Joseph, leading to incredible results in his *personal, family* and *professional* lives. What does this say about your own dungeon experience? While I don't wish to speak breezily about your own time in a personal prison cell, we can say one thing: Follow Joseph's pattern while the word of the Lord is testing you. Then leave the results in his hands. I believe that you—and perhaps many others for generations to come—will be glad that you did.

DYING TO LIVE APPLICATION

Learn to look beyond the walls of experiences which temporarily imprison you.

QUESTIONS FOR REFLECTION

Do you have, or have you ever had, a dungeon-like experience in your life?

What caused it? Did it seem fair? Were you resentful, depressed or beaten down? What helped you get through that cramped, restricted or frightening period?

Did you eventually benefit from this experience? How? Did anyone else?

CHAPTER 16

✠ ✠ ✠

The Choice

A life preserved is lost. A life invested is kept. These axioms are woven into the fabric of all we have considered in *Dying to Live*. The staggering stories of men and women who died to live oxygenate every biography we have encountered. For example, we stood in the shadows of Abraham's life, and even God seemed to be in awe of Abraham's willingness to sacrifice Isaac. Those who refuse to cloak their lives in their own interests, extend them for the sake of longevity without meaning, or hold onto what is impossible to keep tower over their circumstances and the "cold and timid souls who know neither victory or defeat."[120]

The overarching idea that plays like background music in every chapter is that our lives are expendable commodities for God's grand plan—however cruel, irrational or inexplicable it may seem at times. *Purpose, process* and *results* come up again and again when we choose to *die to live*.

- God's *purpose* for working out his plan means following in the footsteps of Jesus, who "humbled himself by becoming obedient to the point of death, even death on a cross" (Phil. 2:8b).

---

120   Memorable Quotes and quotations from Theodore Roosevelt, http://www.memorable-quotes.com/theodore+roosevelt,a589.html

- We are faced with the heavy *process* of having our outer lives degraded, stripped away, or rotted in the darkness when we fall into the ground in submission. When the outer husk of our lives is removed, the kernel of the life of God is free to flower like a miraculous stalk of grain.

- How can we describe the *results*, consequences or harvest for our lives? What words come to mind? Here is a start: freedom from the sickly bonds of routine human living, fulfillment, the long view, meaning, nobility, value, love, legacy, sacrifice for the highest ends, victory beyond terrible or temporary costs, immortality, vision that sees beyond the lesser and the trivial, passion that burns like a fire that cannot be extinguished, commitment or devotion that survives the spilling of life blood and entry into the ageless journals of heroism, astounding results for others. You can add your own descriptors.

It doesn't make any difference whether it was Elijah who fell down, helpless, inert and exhausted under the juniper tree; Daniel and his three friends; Esther or Joan of Arc; Jacob at Peniel, or any of the other characters. The *purpose* of God was shrouded in the mists of his own design, the *process* was at work, and the *results* will stand like mountain peaks above the clouds of human history.

"He is no fool who gives what he cannot keep to gain that which he cannot lose"[121] is Jim Elliot's immortal statement before he was martyred along with his four friends on January 8, 1956. They lost their lives in a hail of Auca (Waodani) spears on the banks of the Curaray River.

---

121   Jim Elliot Quote, Billy Graham Center Archives, Wheaton College, http://www.wheaton.edu/bgc/archives/faq/20.htm.

The lives of these intelligent, rugged athletes from Wheaton College could almost surely have been saved had they chosen to use the weapons they had brought with them. They could have returned to their wives and children and continued their missionary careers. Instead, they chose not to defend themselves against these Aucas (the very name is pejorative and carries the idea of bloodthirsty enemies), whom they had come to invite to receive eternal life.

In the blip of time after landing their Piper PA-14 on the dangerous riverbank runway, they had no opportunity to reflect on what was happening in front of them. They embodied Romans 5:10: "while we were enemies we were reconciled to God by the death of his Son." These five men were similarly ready to die, if need be, so that those who might be called their enemies could be forgiven by God. This commitment to die even as they lived cost the lives of some of the choicest young men in their generation. By God's grace, many of these *enemies* of God and everybody else have become saintly models themselves. They now follow in the footsteps of those they murdered.

Losing what they could not save except for a few years–their lifespans–the so-called "Ecuador Five" were planted in death. These sown lives resulted in shock and loss around the Christian world, yet led to an incredible spiritual harvest.

While most of us are not facing martyrdom, we do face a death trap. We are locked into our temporal realities. Listen again to this summary of Origen: "The greatest challenge we face is not lack of belief but the enormous gravity of our egocentric desires. The weight of these desires creates a force on human nature that is virtually impossible to escape."[122]

---

122   Foster and Beebe, *Longing for God*, 23.

We have traveled with those who in one way or another journeyed to their death but now live immortally. Paraphrasing Evelyn Underhill, they accepted lovelessness for the sake of Love, Nothingness for the sake of All; died without any sure promise of life, forfeited what they had hoped to find. They saw with amazement the foundations of the life that had been theirs crumble in a darkness that held no promise of a dawn. Underhill said that such people bring a

> fresh outbirth of spiritual vitality into the world . . . each of them [are] the founders of spiritual families, centres wherefrom radiates new transcendental life. The "flowing light of the Godhead" is focussed [sic] in them, as in a lens, only that it may pass through them to spread out on every side . . . They have not shrunk from the sufferings of the cross. They have faced the darkness of the tomb. Beauty and agony alike have called them: alike have awakened a heroic response. For them the winter is over: the time of the singing of birds is come.[123]

Underhill's observation shines through in every story we have in this book. Fresh outbursts of spiritual vitality continue to flow from each of their lives.

Many of us feel that we have scarcely graduated from the training wheels of spiritual experience, but we must recognize that the life of the Eternal One is at work. A principle from the life of Joseph, whom we considered in the last chapter, underscores this overriding reality and concludes our study.

In the great Genesis vision Joseph received as a young man, God revealed that he should be supreme among his brothers

---

123   Underhill, *Mysticism*, 516, 539.

and even (counterculturally) his parents as well. All of them would bow before him, youngster though he was. Yet instead of living into this resplendent future, he found himself a slave in Egypt. On the false whim of his master Potiphar's wife, he descended as a foreigner (whose life was very cheap) into the hopelessness of a dungeon.

We have already seen how the commentary on this incident in Psalm 105:19 can illuminate our own dismal experiences: "The word of the LORD tested him." Joseph sat in his dungeon, trapped between two extremes. God's irreversible vision promised spectacular supremacy. His circumstances, however, seemingly had locked him into a hopeless life.

So Joseph had a choice. He could either believe the plan that God had revealed for his life or the reality of his circumstances. His circumstances said that God's vision was a lie. Which was he to believe–the vision or his circumstances? This kind of dichotomy in his sense-deprived environment could have had led to a mental breakdown. Thank God, it didn't for Joseph.

Have you had a great vision for your life? Have you seen the vistas stretching out before you as part of what you assumed was God's plan? But have they become like Amos' basket of summer fruit–sweet, wholesome, healthy, luscious, but now rotted?[124] Instead of singing a beautiful life song, you are wailing in your dungeon, with only your basket of spoiled fruit in front of you.

Evelyn Underhill says John of the Cross has a word for this.

> …in this place of darkness and quietude, this "Night of the Spirit," as St. John of the Cross has called it, you are to dwell there meekly; asking nothing, seeking nothing,

---

124   Amos 8:1-3.

but with your doors flung wide open towards God. And as you do thus, there will come to you an ever clearer certitude that this darkness enveils the goal for which you have been seeking from the first.[125]

John of the Cross endured his own literal dungeon stint, one so severe that he almost died.

If dark periods are ahead for *us*–times of despair, dying, deprivation of all that is meaningful or a daily diet of discouragement–we must remember that whatever we endure, even to death, is not and cannot be the *final* end. The Apostle Paul tells us that our worst and most restrictive times are not worthy to be compared with the glory that is to be revealed to us.[126]

When we bottom out in a dungeon, we need to remember that there is a top to come. The bottom–the dungeon–has a measurable base. The top doesn't.

"What no eye has seen,
   what no ear has heard,
and what no human mind has conceived"—
   the things God has prepared for those who love him.[127]

What God has prepared for us is beyond our ability to compute—especially when all we can see is the dungeon.

When my university professor commented that the Joseph short story is considered one of the most outstanding in all of literature, the word *short* stands out in my mind. Relative to Joseph's whole life, his period in the dungeon *was* short. In

---

125   Evelyn Underhill, *Practical Mysticism: A Little Book for Normal People* (New York: E. P. Dutton & Co., 1914; repr., New York: Cosimo Classics, 2006), 125.

126   Rom. 8:18.

127   1 Cor. 2:9 NIV.

comparison to his eventual career in which he provided a place for his incubating nation, his dungeon despair was brief. In comparison to his life–one of the greatest recorded anywhere– the tormented time early in his Egypt exile was a mere blip on his life screen. For some, of course, a dungeon may restrict us for the rest of our lives. No matter. In light of eternity, we are called to choose God's bigger and broader perspective.

Our considerations in traversing this book have driven us to climb beyond our normal comfort zones. And, by God's grace, we can look at our lives differently and hold them a little more loosely. We can now step back and see them more objectively. We have learned (or re-learned) that they are:

- A *quantity* to be intentionally measured (Psalm 90:12);
- An invaluable *entity* that can't be saved unless it is lost (Mark 8:35-37); and
- A *commodity* to be expended for a priceless purpose (Acts 20:24).

Dying to live is the only reasonable way forward for follow-ers of Christ. The results will far surpass any we could obtain by clutching at our lives as if they are our own.

So whatever territory we must traverse, let's get there! Let us die to live for the glory of God, for the lives of others and for a future that we don't even have the categories or the lan-guage to describe. And . . . may the wind of God blow at your back, as the Celts would say, until you *arrive*–finally whole, finally wholly blessed, and finally completely alive.

Amen.

Charles Haley is founder of Life Serve, Ltd.

The mission of Life Serve is to help Christian leaders in the marketplace reach life goals, spiritually, professionally, and personally.

Clients are served through a broad range of services anchored by the mentoring process. Mentoring "brings a range of gifts, skills, and materials within a program for spiritual growth and life formation" (Leech).

Listening, addressing the big issues that determine success or failure, and providing leveraged opportunities for spiritual formation and life development characterize the Life Serve Mentoring Program.

Life Serve Ltd.
www.lifeserveltd.com
cwh@churchbuilding.com

Other books by the author include:

Beyond Leadership to Destiny—Jacob's Lifetime Journey with God (Spiritual Formation for Third Millennium Leaders)
An Evangelical's Road Less Traveled—A Contemplative Life

Made in the USA
Charleston, SC
27 July 2011